7 Pursuits to Visualize, Realize & Actualize the goals of Human life

Seven-Ps of Human Beings

BINAY KUMAR JHA

First Published in August 2020

ISBN: 978-81-946981-6-6

BLUEROSE PUBLISHERS

www.bluerosepublishers.com

info@bluerosepublishers.com

+91 8882 898 898

Cover Design:

Mohd Arif

Typographic Design:

Tanya Raj Upadhyay

Distributed by: BlueRose, Amazon, Flipkart, Shopclues

Dedication

This book is dedicated to the humanity based professionalism where being human and its usefulness really mean a lot.

About the Book

SEVEN-Ps OF HUMAN BEINGS.

(7 Essential Essence of Human life)

This book is all about Human life describing the **nature, feature**, **need** and **ways of accomplishments** of human beings and its **roles, responsibilities & supporting contributions** towards **Nature, Creature, Humanity, Community, Society** in correlation with **Safety, Health, Environment** (SHE) & **Human Existence** (HE).

Author has explored **seven significant pursuits** of human life that describe all about to feel honoured & proud of being human and to **earn a dignified and respectful livelihood as well.** This work would help to **have pleasurable & enjoyable living, right ways of fulfillment of dreams & desires with accountability & responsibility of a human life.** A co-ordination and correlation between theoretical & practical processes in human life has been visualized with a **blend of spirituality.**

In this book, an effort has been made to express the feelings & experiences in own words of the author with an intention to share some of **life's essential essence** based on the author's personal experiences. **This book would help to be a better person and a result oriented professional ensuring high management skills with holistic approach.**

This book contains concept narratives based on practical knowledge & ideas to **add values** in human lives through sharing knowledge & experiences so gained by the author during the entire tenure of working in various work cultures in various geographical regions of the world at higher management positions in organisations of high reputes in India and abroad.

About the Author

The author of this book is having **four decades** of multifaceted versatile experience in working with organisations of high reputes in India and abroad at senior management positions.

From huge experiences of versatility, the author passionately extracted the essential essence of human life and narrated in his own words to share the same with people who believe in enhancing the knowledge through sharing. The **huge experiences include deliveries of responsibilities towards developing Human values through imparting training & personality development workshops and motivational speeches on moral & ethical value systems in life.**

In spite of having engineering background and working experiences in steel industry, auto components manufacturing industries, infrastructural products related plastic and concrete industries, various projects & service industries; Also, author has rich experiences on working towards **conservation of natural resources through training & motivational workshops and welfare activities based on the implementation of international concepts and standards relate to SHE & HE (Safety Health Environment and Human Existence).**

Author is intended to share the key features of his experiences to the interested people who really honor others' ideas and believe in sharing them on the concept that **Sharing always enhances the knowledge and multiply ideas. This can be expressed as X plus anything is more than X.**

In mathematical format it can be illustrated as (**X+ anything >X**).

Prologue

Before diving into the topics, all respected readers are requested to prepare their mind through the following processes:-

1. Awake your person,
2. Discipline your habits,
3. Organize your time,
4. Determine your purpose,
5. Cultivate your interest,
6. Concentrate your mind,
7. Initiate your ride.

Vision

Being **successful** is **good achievements** for personal & professional performance in life, but being **useful** for the humanity is **great attainment** to meet the purpose of life. Based on this ethos, the vision of this work is

- Understanding the purpose of human life,
- Awakening for the inner power of human beings,
- Aspiring for the big dreams,
- Inspiring for the absolute success,
- Enabling for achievements,
- Strengthening the belief level,
- Enhancing the usefulness of being human.

Mission

- To share the concepts ideas to the people to be useful more than the successful.
- To create values for performance more than the physical wealth.
- To enable people to be more vigilant and a good human being.
- To cultivate good practices to create good moral values.
- To help people to lead a life of pleasure and purposeful.
- To create a sense of responsibility and inspiration for great deeds.

Preface

When **Mother Nature** became matured with its entire establishment and aura of infinite energy in all respect in all aspects and needed to be nurtured and maintained, the new species were created as **Human beings.**

The species consisting of wisdom, talent and ability to create thoughts are full of all features that can understand purpose of creation of human life and can act to achieve the same.

Human beings are considered the most significant creation of nature, sufficiently equipped with in built strength and capabilities to accept the most difficult challenges and convert them into big achievements through inventions, innovations, and researches to keep & maintain the world as the most convenient place to live a pleasurable life on the principle of live & let live.

Existence of human beings is based on some principles and basic essential ethics to enjoy the essence of life.

All contents and narratives are personal view points for sharing and enjoying purposes, not to be quoted and compared with any similar thoughts or contents in any ways. This is purely based on personal experience and not subject to any dispute or conflicts in any ways at any point of time.

CONTENTS

THE 1ST P- PURPOSE OF HUMAN LIFE.

(Almighty shows His omnipotence through human beings)

Human the most significant, dignified and powerful species of the universe has been created for the specific purpose. When **Mother Nature** became matured with its entire establishment and aura of infinite energy in all respect in all aspects and required to be nurtured and maintained, the most intelligent species were created as **Human beings.**

The species consisting of intelligence, wisdom, talent and ability to create thoughts are full of all features that can understand purpose of creation of human life and can act to achieve the same.

When we discuss about the human life, the three certain events **Birth, Living & Death** comes into picture. These are realities of life. All of us are gifted with great mystery of life that is our living in the world, but the big question

WHAT IS THE PURPOSE OF HUMAN LIFE? Is it simply to live, to work, and to die or there is something more to it? When we grow up-to a few years of age, we begin to experience and realise the facts and realities of the world. We undergo some rituals and gradually become influenced by some beliefs & faiths. Then the element religion comes in life through family, society and surroundings we belong to and live in.

Though the human beings as a species initially were not much different than an animal and they evolved gradually through the utilization of their intelligence, wisdom & talents. Over a period human beings developed and differentiated themselves from other creatures of the planet earth and a new culture of living started. As the culture grew gradually, the unique thoughts of each individual started to develop distinct style of living as per individual convenience in consideration with various affecting factors like geographical region, availability of food items and supporting natural resources in establishing livelihood. This practice gave birth to different civilizations and various ways of livings and livelihood in various parts of the earth.

Afterwards, different languages came into existence based on natural sounds received, grasped and understood in their own ways in the different geographical regions and lingual communication started in different ways.

Over a period when Human beings became more civilized and well established, the **person of each individual** got awakened and then personal interests came into picture. But at the same time, human beings were in habits of living together to fulfill each other's need & greed and share feelings, the concept of society came into picture based on likeminded thoughts, livings, and habits. Then gradually concepts of secured & established living with ownerships emotions were developed and resulted into following format of present existence in the world.

Person →Family →Society →Village / Township →Region→Country → Continents.

Now the human beings developed with senses of possessiveness of personal and social belongings. They began to take good care of their body for the sake of domestic, social, and political well-being. Intellectually, they have made strident advancements. They explored the earth, oceans, and space. To set right all in order and peaceful living, some institutions were formed and established like marriage, cultural & educational institutions, and induced celebrations & festivals to enjoy pleasurable & peaceful life etc.

Strangely enough, with all his achievements, human being remains ignorant about the prime source of energy from which his body and mind drive their strength – soul- his true self.

Human beings have so much identified with the body that they are unable to distinguish their soul from the body. With changing world, Human-beings began to think the material things as source of happiness and technology as an integral part of life in present circumstances creates illusions to happiness through consistent injecting and persistent infecting marketing advertisement on material things.

Human beings are supposed & considered the most significant creation of nature, sufficiently equipped with in built strength and capabilities to accept the most difficult challenges and convert them into big achievements through inventions, innovations, and researches to keep & maintain the world as the most convenient place to live a pleasurable life on the principle of **live & let live.**

Existence of human beings is based on some principles and basic essential ethics to enjoy the essence of life with accountability and responsibility towards nature and all creatures as well. Human beings have the responsibility to follow the principles of

→ Walk together,
→ Work together,
→ Live together and
→ Love each other.

This would be the best purpose rather ultimate purpose of human life to implement in day to day routine.

Many people believe in the **principle of Karma & law of retribution.** Being human, we have intellects & discretionary power **(Vivek),** so that we can decide something to do or not to do, we can choose to the karma followed by destiny. Other creatures cannot choose or change anything; they just have to go through the life granted. Therefore the purpose, the sense of Human life is greater.

The act of eating, sleeping, and creating children can be performed by animals as well, but Human beings are supposed to do something else out of these routine functions. Humans have more obligations and greater purposes in life. They are supposed to gain **Devine knowledge → Atmagyan →Self-realization.** If one dies without this, he would be supposed failed the purpose of his life. In other words, we can define Atmagyan as superior wisdom that can tell about the absolute truth along with appropriate significance of all belongings, relationships. Purpose of human life is to understand the existence of supreme power that derives the universe and greater purpose is to know the duties to perform towards this nature, creatures, colleagues and relatives in right proportion without expecting any returns. A human is essentially supposed to be good enough & absolute loyal to his creator and creations but when he gains divine knowledge and helps other human beings also to gain the same divinity by transferring knowledge then he becomes Guru, the Great human being. No individual in the universe is created equally, the destiny guides which we call it Karma.

Devine knowledge guides us to be compassionate towards all living beings and love all living beings. This means do not be envious or hateful of others. Be friendly to others, be nice to others, be kind to others, be generous to others, be merciful to others, and be charitable to the needy. A human being must realise the aim of his life. One should believe the almighty makes the passage for all in this world with turbulence not more than his capability.

The omnipotence & supremacy of nature has incorporated all its power in human beings to be omniscient and find & realize the omnipresence of super power through which the whole universe is driven.

GOD has created all human beings unique and distinct to get various infinite new things to happen through their thoughts generated by unique dreams and distinct hunches got from the nature. The types and quality of dreams for each person depends on the individual talent & capability to deliver. Thoughts are things and can be converted into realities in physical forms.

GOD creates opportunities and plant into human mind in the form of dreams and thoughts through hunches and wants to be delivered by Human beings and the purpose of human beings would be fulfilled.

Scientifically, human beings are different from other beings on the earth by their genetic codes. What makes a human being unique from other beings is their ability to think rationally, make relationships and connections. Human beings have unique superiority over other beings on the earth.

Human beings are not only able to think rationally, which other beings cannot, but we are able and have the power of using that knowledge and implementing those thoughts to reach the highest level of accomplishment and success.

There are many interpretations about the sentence “What does it mean to be human?” People around the world have different answers and point of views regarding this question. **Albert Einstein, German born American Physicist, believes that human being means “The most important human endeavor is the striving for morality in our actions. Our inner balance and even our very existence depend on it.**

Only morality in our actions can give beauty and dignity to life.” This Subjective fact could be human behavior and as a matter of fact I believe there is not only one accurate meaning for the word “human”.

On the other hand being a human means to have the **ability to differentiate between right and wrong.** One should be able to know how ethical and appropriate a decision is. A human does not have to accept whatever he is told so, he rather be able by himself to know the right.

Being a human means having the ability to think rationally and critically. As a human, they do have these abilities, but since they are not able to use them, I believe there is no difference between them and animals. They should be able to think deeply beyond the critical tangible things in the world.

Everybody knows that tangible aspects such as driving car, building roads, painting and the arts make us different from animals, but what we have to understand the critical and an important point.

We, as human beings, are able to make relationships and connections. This unique superiority helps us to broaden and grow our horizons, thrive success and makes our species proud of what we are.

In addition, everybody has different definition, beliefs and thought of what does it mean to be human. We were sent to this world with responsibilities and purpose. We have superiority over other beings; we are able to think rationally and deeply. We have the ability to differentiate right from wrong.

Our lives depend on what we think? What we decide? And how we decide? How we use our natural skills of making decision and make the best choice. We have not fulfilled our responsibilities and have not proven ourselves as responsible human beings. We, as humans, are supposed to make relationships and connections with each other. We have to respect and accept morality and have to prove ourselves as responsible creation.

Human beings have inbuilt three main constituents

1. **Mind** (Receives hunches, dreams and creates thoughts.)
2. **Body** (Acts and functions as per thoughts created in mind.)
3. **Soul** (Feels & realizes pleasure, anguish and express emotions to control the right things rightly.)

It is imperative to have vertical alignment of mind, body and soul for right results in right directions. Vertical alignment means the perfect adjustment of thoughts & action with emotions & realizations.

Vertical alignment of Mind, Body & Soul may be illustrated as per following sketch.

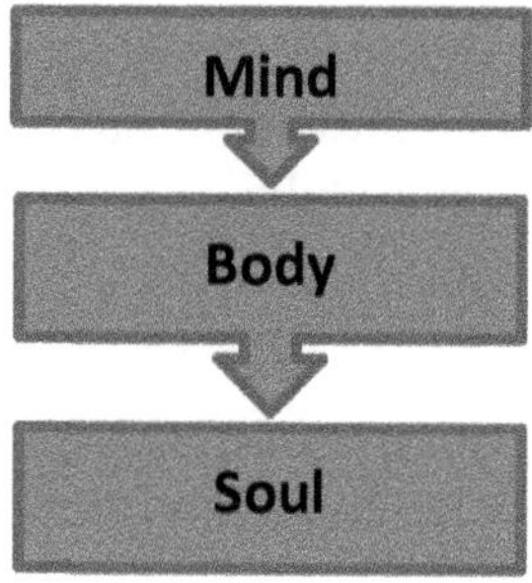

Consciously or not, directly or indirectly, in the short or in the long term, whatever we do, whatever we hope, whatever we dream, somehow, is related to a deep profound desire for **absolute happiness.**

Let us view the following **Happiness pyramid.**

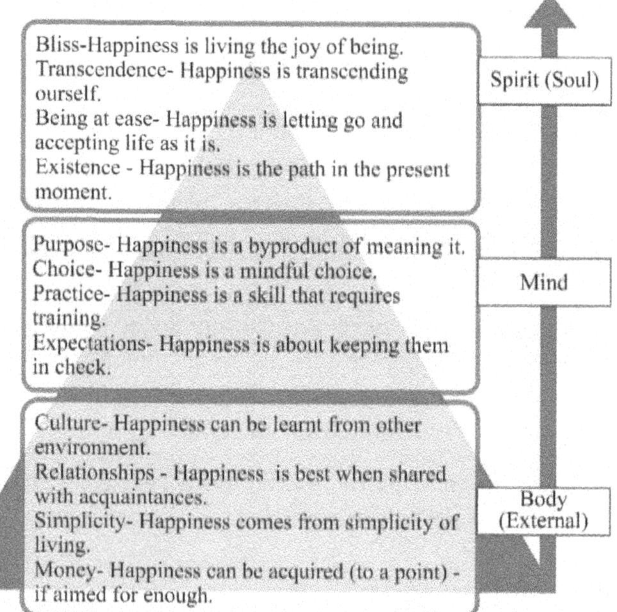

Above happiness pyramid is a definition of Happiness in totality produced, realized and controlled by the three integral constituents of Human beings in their life.

GOD has provided five senses to help & support the human beings to feel & experience the existence & presence of themselves along-with other visible, invisible, material, celestial things in and around them. Five senses are named as follows:-

1. Sight- Eyes
2. Smell- Nose
3. Hearing- Ears
4. Taste- Tongue
5. Touch- Skin

The sensing organs associated with each sense send information to the brain to understand and perceive the world around us.

These all senses are inbuilt in almost all creatures but humans have its significance more than the other ones because human can think, interpret and analyze the things. Humans can judge the things, understand the situations / circumstances well, take decisions in accordance with the prevailing circumstances.

The sense of space→In addition to the traditional big five, there is another sense that deals with how brain understands the existence & presence of the body in space. This sense is called ***proprioception.***

Additional senses & variations→there are more-subtle senses that most people never really perceive. For example, there are neuron sensors that sense movement to control balance and the tilt of the head. Specific kinesthetic receptors exist for detecting stretching in muscles and tendons, helping people to keep track of their limbs. Other receptors detect levels of oxygen in certain arteries of the bloodstream.

Sometimes, people do not even perceive senses the same way. People with synesthesia can see sounds as colors or associate certain sights with smells, for example.

Proprioception includes the sense of movement and position of our limbs and muscles. For example, proprioception enables a person to touch their finger to the tip of their nose even with their eyes closed. It enables a person to climb steps without looking at each one. People with poor proprioception may be clumsy an uncoordinated.

Law of nature is **POGU** (Permanent Ongoing Growing Unlimited) and **Change is the constant function of nature.** People became more developed and began to think all round continuous improvement with vested interests for convenience & conduciveness.

Let us have a look in the hidden meaning in a word **watch.** Normally the word watch means to observe carefully, but what to observe mostly is defined in the word itself if we consider this word as an abbreviation and expanding as follows:-

W-Words
A-Actions
T- Time
C-Character
H-Health

These above five most significant elements of human life define and decide the purpose of life in true sense.

It would be pertinent to remember the following phrases mentioned here under.

- → Watch your words as they are likely to be your thoughts,
- → Watch your thoughts as they are likely to be your actions,
- → Watch your actions as they are likely to be your habits,
- → Watch your habits as they are likely to be your destiny,

"So man is maker of his fate".

This is very important to mention that thoughts & actions need determination and suitable direction to go ahead. Right thoughts and actions in accordance with the same in right direction would certainly bear the right desired results.

Each of us is unique. No one has ever existed like us or ever will. We are each unique expressions of human life, and that is a wonderful thing. It means we are all capable of doing something that no one has ever or will ever be able to do. That thing represents our passion, and it's what will give each of us the life of our dreams.

To lead a life of **ethical integrity** is one of the most significant purposes of life and it must be responded well to the challenge the life presents.

Such a challenge cannot be made better when "it has been narrowed, simplified, and bowdlerized by others in advance"

This defense of the endorsement constraint grounds it in a background conception of a good human life, one that holds that the goodness of a human life lies in "the inherent value of a skilled performance of living

I believe that my purpose is to find that passion and share it with the world to the maximum extent possible.

All purposes of human life are met through purity and perfection. Perfection comes through persistent practices with patience and consistent efforts.

Highlights

- *Faith never fails*
- *Faith & fear do not exist at a time*
- *A human being is a toy of God, we must keep playing.*
- *God gives, gives, and forgives; Man gets, gets, and forgets.*
- *He, who fears he will suffer, already suffers because he fears."*
- *Man says, show me and I will trust you, God says, trust me and I will show you.*
- *Life is never made unbearable by circumstances, but only by lack of meaning and purpose.*
- *Challenges are what make life interesting and overcoming them is what makes life meaningful.*
- *Take risks in your life. If you win, you can lead, if you lose, you can guide.*
- *Meaningful death is better than a meaningless life.*
- *We are not created by default; we are in this world for some purpose.*

→For those serious about bringing a positive holistic change in their life may turn out to be the most rewarding enterprise one can ever undertake.

→The author is available in person to impart effective & result oriented training & workshops on demand.

THE 2ND P- PERSONALITY

(Personality is the signature of a person)

All human beings are unique by human values, nature, features, potential, and physique. These all inclusively make a person different and distinct entity that signifies **personality**.

Personality may be defined as the characteristic sets of behaviors, cognitions, and emotional patterns that evolve from biological and environmental factors. Some theories focus on motivation and psychological interactions with one's environment. Trait-based personality theories define personality as the traits that predict a person's behavior.

On the other hand, more behaviorally-based approaches define personality through learning and habits. Nevertheless, most theories view personality as relatively stable.

The study of the psychology of personality, called personality psychology, attempts to explain the tendencies that underlie differences in behavior. Many approaches have been taken on to study personality, including biological, cognitive, learning and trait-based theories, as well as psychodynamic, and humanistic approaches.

As per study, it has been observed that the personality traits are more malleable by environmental influences than researchers originally believed rather; personality differences predict the occurrence of life experiences.

One study that has shown how the home environment, specifically the types of parents a person has, can affect and shape their personality.

Parenting plays vital roles in building personality traits with different styles and behaviours in babies. Children who were securely attached tend to be more trusting, sociable, and are confident in their day-to-day life. Children who were disorganized were reported to have higher levels of anxiety, anger, and risk-taking behavior.

It is found that personality is not stable over the course of a lifetime, but it changes much more quickly during childhood, so personality constructs in children are referred to as temperament. Temperament is regarded as the precursor to personality. The personality theorists consider temperament EAS (Emotionality, Activity, and Sociability).

Personality Measurement, Types & Category - Personality can be determined through a variety of tests. Due to the fact that personality is a complex idea, the dimensions of personality and scales of personality tests vary. There are two main tools commonly used to measure personality.

1. **Objective tests-** An objective test is a psychological test that measures an individual's characteristics in a way that is not influenced by the examiner's own beliefs. In this way, they are said to be independent of rater bias. Objective items include multiple choice, true false, matching and completion etc. Objective tests generally explore an individual's conscious thoughts and feelings. It is self-report measures, relies on an individual's personal responses and is relatively free of rater bias.

2. **Projective measures-** Projective measures are founded in psychoanalytic theories of personality and involve using ambiguous stimuli to reveal inner aspects of an individual's personality. It lets a person to respond presumably revealing hidden emotions, internal attitudes, traits, behavior patterns and internal conflicts projected by the person into test.

A recent, well-known, measuring tool that psychologists use is the 16PF. It measures personality based on 16 factor theory of personality. Psychologists also use it as a clinical measuring tool to diagnose psychiatric disorders and help with prognosis and therapy planning.

In this method, **8 categories of personality are defined as E,F,I,J,N,P,S,T** based on observations through four main questions and some sub questions related to the main questions (as mentioned below) are asked and natural behaviours of the person are noticed and the observations are noted down while answering. For each question, there would be two probable observations / behaviours while answering and the suitable category is defined.

Q- 1. Is he outwardly / inwardly focused? If the observation is:-

Could be described as talkative, outgoing.	Could be described as reserved, private.
Likes to be in a fast-paced environment.	Prefers a slower pace with time for contemplation.
Tends to work out ideas with others, think out loud.	Tends to think things through inside head.
Enjoys being the center of attention.	Would rather observe than be the center of attraction.
Then this would be in **"E"** category.	Then this would be in **"I"** category
E - Extraversion	**I – Introversion**

Q – 2. How does he prefer to take information? If the observation is:-

Focus on the reality on how things are.	Imagines the possibilities of how things could be.
Pays attention to concrete facts and details.	Notices the big picture, sees how everything connects.
Prefers ideas that have practical applications.	Enjoys ideas and concepts for his own sake.
Likes to describe things in a specific literal way.	Likes to describe things in a figurative, poetic way.
Then this would be in **"S" category.**	Then this would be in **"N" category.**
S- Sensing	**N- Intuition**

Q – 3. **How does he prefer to make decisions? If the observation is:-**

Makes decisions in an impersonal way, using logical reasoning.	Base of his decisions on personal values and how his actions affect others.
Values justice, fairness.	Values harmony, forgiveness.
Enjoys finding the flaws in an argument.	Likes to please others and point out the best in people.
Could be described as reasonable, level headed.	Could be described as warm empathy.
Then this would be in **"T" category.**	Then this would be in **"F" category.**
T- Thinking	**F – Feeling**

Q – 4. **How does he prefer to live his outer life? If the observation is:-**

Prefers to have matters settled.	Prefers to leave his options open.
Thinks rules and deadlines should be respected.	Sees rules and deadlines as flexible.
Prefers to have detailed step by step instructions.	Likes to improvise and make things up as he goes.
Makes plans an interested to know what he is getting into.	Is spontaneous, enjoy surprises and new situations.
Then this would be in **"J" category.**	Then this would be in **"P" category.**
J- Judging	**P – Perceiving**

After categorization as above, 16 types of personalities are defined through permutation and combination of the categories considering with some common aspects.

Let us study the following matrix is the illustration of the 16PF tool in sequential order of %age availability in descending order.

S.N.	**Type**	**Special Charecteristics**	**Nature / Behaviour**	**%**
1	ISFJ I-Introversion, S- Sensing, F- Feeling, J- Judging.	*MOST LOYAL, *A HIGH SENSE OF DUTY	Amiable, Warm, Considerate, Gentle, Responsible, Pragmatic, Thorough, Devoted caretakers, Accountable, Ready to sacrifice, Prefers doing work behind the scene and enjoy being helpful to others.	13.8

2	ESFJ E-Extraversion, S-Sensing, F-Feeling, J- Judging.	*MOST HARMONIZING, *HOST & HOSTESSES OF THE WORLD,	Appropriate, Gracious, Conscientious, Organized, Practical, Good interpersonal skills, Thoughtful, Friendly, Reliable, Enjoy being active & productive, Eager to please others,	12.3
3	ISTJ I-Introversion, S-Sensing, T-Thinking, J-Judging.	*MOST RESPONSIBLE, *DOING WHAT SHOULD BE DONE,	Responsible, Sincere, Analytical, Reserved, Realistic, Systematic, Practical, Private, Hardworking, Trustworthy, Compulsive, Follow Rules & Regulations.	11.6
4	ISFP I-Introversion, S-Sensing, F-Feeling, P-Perceiving.	*MOST ARTISTIC, *SEES MUCH BUT SHARES LITTLE,	Gentle, Warm, Sensitive, Nurturing, Helpful, Flexible, Short range planner, Nature loving, Good team member, Seek to create a personal environment that is both beautiful & practical, Unassuming.	8.8

5	ESTJ E-Extraversion, S-Sensing, T-Thinking, J-Judging.	*MOST HARD CHARGING, *LIFE'S ADMINISTRATORS,	Efficient, Outgoing, Analytical, Systematic, Structured, Sociable, Realistic, Result driven, Producer, Traditional. Opinionated, Like to run the show and get things done in an orderly fashion.	8.7
6	ESFP E-Extraversion, S-Sensing, F-Feeling, P-Perceiving.	*MOST GENEROUS, *ONLY GOES AROUND ONCE IN LIFE.	Sociable, Spontaneous, Loves surprises, Playful, Enthusiastic, Friendly, Tactful, Have strong common sense, Enjoy helping people in tangible way, cuts red tape, Juggles multiple projects/events, Quip master.	8.5
7	ENFP E-Extraversion, N-Intuition, F-Feeling, P-Perceiving.	*MOST OPTIMISTIC, *GIVING LIFE AN EXTRA SQUEEZE,	Enthusiastic, People oriented, Creative, spontaneous, Seeks harmony, supportive, Value inspiration, See potential in others, Playful, Life of Party, More starts than finishes.	8.1

8	ISTP I- Introversion, S-Sensing, T-Thinking, P- Perceiving.	*MOST PRAGMATIC, *READY TO TRY ANYTHING ONCE,	Action oriented, Analytical, Independent, Very observant, Enjoy adventure, Cool and aloof, Hands-on practicality, Spontaneou, Unpretentious, Skilled at understanding how mechanical things work, Ready to face what happens.	5.4
9	INFP I- Introversion, N-Intuition, F-Feeling, P- Perceiving.	*MOST IDEALISTIC, *PERFORMING NOBLE SERVICE TO AID SOCIETY	Sensitive, Creative, Idealistic, Perceptive, Strict personal values, Seeks inner order / peace & harmony, Reserved, Focuses on dreams and possibilities. Non-directive.	4.4
10	ESTP E- Extraversion , S-Sensing, T-Thinking, P- Perceiving.	*MOST SPONTANEOUS *THE ULTIMATE REALIST	Unconventional approach, Fun loving, Gregarious, versatile, Curious, Realistic, Lives for here and now, Action oriented Skillful negotiator &Good problem solving.	4.3

11	INTP I- Introversion, N-Intuition, T-Thinking, P- Perceiving.	*MOST CONCEPTUAL *A LOVE OF PROBLEM SOLVING	Intellectual, Logical, Precise, Reserved, Imaginative, original thinkers who enjoy speculation, Challenges others to think, Absent-minded professor, Competency needs, Socially cautious. Flexible.	3.3
12	ENTP E- Extraversion , N-Intuition, T-Thinking, P- Perceiving.	*MOST INVENTIVE *ONE EXITING CHALLENGE AFTER ANOTHER	Inventive, Inquisitive, Strategic, versatile, Enthusiastic, Enterprising, Argues both sides of a point to learn, Enjoy new ideas and challenges, Value inspiration.	3.2
13	ENFJ E- Extraversion , N-Intuition, F-Feeling, J- Judging.	*MOST PERSUASIVE *SMOOTH TALKING PERSUADER	Charismatic, Diplomatic, Compassionate, Caring, Organized, Idealistic, Responsible, Ignores unpleasant, Skilled communicators who value connection with people.	2.5

14	INTJ I-Introversion, N-Intuition, T-Thinking, J-Judging.	*MOST INDEPENDENT *EVERYTHING HAS ROOM FOR IMPROVEMENT	Innovative, Independent, Strategic, Theory based & skeptical thinking, Sees world as chessboard, Driven by their own original ideas to achieve improvements, High need for competency, My way thinking.	2.1
15	ENTJ E-Extraversion, N-Intuition, T-Thinking, J-Judging.	*MOST COMMANDING *LIFE'S NATURAL LEADERS	Ambitious, Argumentative, Gregarious, Visionary, System planners, Low tolerance for Incompetency, Independent, Effective organizers of people and long range planner. Takes Charge.	1.8
16	INFJ I-Introversion, N-Intuition, F-Feeling, J- Judging.	*MOST CONTEMPLATIVE *AN INSPIRATION TO OTHERS	Reflective, Introspective, Quietly caring, Creative, Linguistically gifted, Psychic, Idealistic, Organized, Dependable, Gentle, Compassionate, Seek harmony and co-operation, Enjoy intellectual stimulation.	1.5

Personality Development (Aspects, Stages & Traits) - Personality Development is the process by which attributes, attitudes and pattern of behaviours are developed in an individual. Things that support into making an individual unique and different from others are personality development. There are several things to be considered when we talk about personality development as there are no two individuals that are the same. We may look the same and may have had similar experiences in life but we are all unique in our own ways. Our reactions and personality development process would be different. People who are brought up in the same household will develop their own peculiar pattern of reacting and responding various situations they face.

The attributes of a person make him or her special but there are various factors that contribute to the type of personality that is formed. These are temperament, environment and character and they may have a negative or positive effect on personality development.

There are a lot of factors that have gone into the development of a particular type of personality. From childhood to adulthood, we go through a lot of process, experiences and situations that all contribute to the formation of our personality.

These have all played a role in making us who and what we are today. We have the capability to become whatever we desire as long we are willing to commit our time, resources and efforts in making it possible.

In this article, I shall be examining the basic aspects of personality development which are referred to as the Big 5. Most experts in the field agree that these are the basic ones.

These five aspects include: Extraversion, Agreeableness, Openness, Conscientiousness, and Neuroticism. Several other theorists have written on several other aspects of personality development, some of which include the Mental aspects, Spiritual aspects, Emotional aspects, Physical aspects, Social aspects, and Moral aspects. These various aspects provide us a different view into the process by which an individual's personality is developed.

Aspects of Personality Development- Theory of big-5 are quite broad and they have a range of other specific traits. They were derived from statistical analysis of the traits which tend to occur when people describe themselves or other people. Sometimes, researchers refer to them as the five- factor theory or five-factor model.

1. Extraversion

This trait describes an individual's outgoing or social attitude. They are sometimes seen as the life of the party and enjoy hanging out with people, going out for social events and are generally full of life and energy. Those who are low in extraversion are less outgoing and prefer to stay by themselves. The introverts have less energy and love to be quiet. The ones who score high in it enjoy relating with people and are enthusiastic about life and very action-oriented. These are extroverts. Various types of jobs require different levels of extraversion and it will be useful in jobs that are related to teaching, sales and general interaction with people.

Each of the Big 5 personality traits is also made up of at least 6 sub traits. Under extraversion, we have: cheerfulness, excited, activity level, assertiveness, gregariousness and friendliness.

2. Agreeableness

This manifests itself in an individual's behaviours that show kindness, sympathy, warmness and consideration for others. Those who score high here are very empathetic with others and accommodate them. They are also positive minded. The ones that score low are selfish and lack empathy. They seem to always be in competition with others and try to manipulate their way through situations instead of co-operating with others. Those with a high score here tend to desire harmonious living and put aside their own interests in order to please others. They believe that people are honest and trustworthy. These individuals will enjoy team building activities and working harmoniously while those that score low would be good scientists, critics or soldiers. The sub-traits here include: sympathy, modesty, co-operation and trust.

3. Openness

This describes the open mindedness of an individual. A person who scores high here will enjoy trying new things. They tend to be imaginative and generally open minded about everything. Others who score low would be close minded and prefer routine. They are resistant to change and would be very analytical. Those with an open mind will also tend to love the arts and think deeply too. An individual with this trait may fit in advertising, research while those who score low would enjoy jobs that require routine work. The sub traits here include: imagination, adventurousness, emotionality, artistic interests, intellect and liberalism.

4. Conscientiousness

This trait describes how an individual controls, regulates and directs their impulses. Individuals who score high with this personality trait tend to have a high level of self-discipline. They always follow a plan instead of acting on the spur of the moment. This makes them successful in their endeavors and able to achieve their goals. They are seen as responsible and reliable. They may also be workaholics and perfectionists which may make them boring and inflexible. The sub traits of this aspect include: achievement-driven, dutifulness, orderliness, self-efficacy, self-discipline and cautiousness. Individuals with this trait will always stay focused on their goals regardless of challenges and obstacles because they believe they will always succeed if they follow their plan. They will be able to fit in across different occupations. Their need for achievement is the constant driving force.

5. Neuroticism

This also means emotional stability. It describes an individual's ability to stay balanced and stable when faced with tough challenges. One who scores high in neuroticism has the tendency to experience negative emotions. On the other hand, those who score high in emotional stability react less emotionally and don't get upset easily. They are usually calm and stable, though it does not mean they experience a lot of positive feelings. Those who are high in neuroticism are emotionally reactive and feel threatened or get into bad moods even in a normal situation. They may also find it difficult to think clearly when they are stressed. Those with high emotional stability are preferred in most professions as they have control over their emotions while those with low stability can be distracted by deadlines, personal situations and pressure. The sub traits here include: anxiety, anger, depression, self-consciousness, vulnerability and immoderation.

Personality Development Stages

There are five main stages in human being as mentioned below when personality development phenomena take place.

1. Infant stage – 2 years

During this stage, the infant begins to learn to trust or not to trust. If well taken care of and loved, will begin to develop a sense of security and have positive outlook to life. If it is also not done properly, it will lead to the infant becoming insecure.

2. Toddler stage – 18 months to 3 years

At this state, the child begins to develop the will. If guided properly, the child begins to have self-confidence. It is not an easy process and the child could be seen as being stubborn.

3. Pre-school stage – 3 years and above

This stage is referred to by some as the 'play age.' The child begins to develop some form of initiative. They also start using their imagination. At this stage they also gradually begin to understand how to lead and follow others.

4. School age stage

At this stage, the child begins to learn formal skills. They begin to know how to relate with their peers and begin to develop basic intellectual skills. The success at this stage in their development will dependent on how the early stages were.

5. Adolescent stage

The child begins to mature at this stage and begins to nurture a set of values which will help them in life. They also begin to understand themselves at this stage.

Personality Development Traits

Mainly three traits are observed in a human being to contribute in personality development processes as mentioned here under.

1. Temperament

Here, we refer to traits that a child comes with into the world which are genetically determined. These traits to a major extent influence the child's approach to the world and how he or she learns in the process. From studies that have been carried out, some of these genes control the nervous system development which also controls behavior.

2. Environment

The environment in which a child grows up affects to a large extent how the personality will eventually be. It is advised that quality parenting be given to help in the proper development of the child.

3. Character

This is formed from the emotional, perceptive and behavioral patterns that are learned by experience and determine how an individual thinks, feels and behaves.

An individual's personality continuously evolves throughout his life but we have seen that much of it is dependent on traits they were born with and experiences they have had through life.

Overall, Personality of a person is very much personal and deciding factor in the achievements of life. Contribution of education and knowledge in personality is very high.

The sum total of qualities, quirks, characteristics, beliefs, attitudes and psychological traits comprises personality. Thus, personality development would involve an enhancement in all the areas of human life. A host of factors like heredity, environment, family and societal conditions play a role in influencing and shaping one's personality. Therefore, one would have to work on all these areas to bring about a well-rounded development.

The whole process may take considerable effort, but it can be started with some easy and effective techniques and a perceptible transformation in whole personality could be observed.

Highlights

- *Personality is the index of person's traits & features.*
- *Personality is the key of performance, achievements and success of life.*
- *Personality is the characteristic sets of behaviors, cognitions, and emotional patterns that evolve from biological and environmental factors.*
- *The sum total of qualities, quirks, characteristics, beliefs, attitudes and psychological traits comprises personality.*
- *Personality can be developed suitably through value addition activities.*
- *Personality Development is the process by which attributes, attitudes and pattern of behaviours are developed in an individual.*

For those serious about bringing a positive holistic change in their life, personality development may turn out to be the most rewarding enterprise one can ever undertake. The author is available in person to impart effective & result oriented workshops on demand.

THE 3RD P- PATIENCE

(Patience is the root of accomplishments)

Let us imagine that we are waiting for someone to finish compiling a report that we need for a meeting. We are already late, we can feel our body getting tensed, and we are starting to get angry.

Suddenly, we lose our temper and yell at the person for putting us behind schedule. We can tell that they're shocked and upset by your outburst, but it can't help it out rather, the delays multiply affecting the quality of the work as well.

We likely all lose our patience occasionally. But doing so frequently or inappropriately can harm our reputation, damage our relationships, increase stress, or escalate a difficult situation. We must adhere that **"Anything that is worth attaining is worth waiting for".**

Patience is the ability to stay calm while waiting for an outcome that we need or want. It is the ability to wait for something without frustration till it is completed or finished with its intended purpose is useful skill and a good aspect of one's personality that is called Patience. Patience is a virtue which fights anger, helps to maintain cool & maintains temperament even in averse situations of anguish.

Patience is the capacity to endure difficult circumstances such as perseverance in the face of delay; tolerance of provocation without responding in annoyance / anger; or forbearance when under strain, especially when faced with longer-term difficulties. Patience is the level of endurance one can have before negativity.

Patience is a measurement of profoundness of personality of a person and defines the sustainability to withstand in the state of mental peace without much anxiety. It is a good feature of a person to be able to tolerate something that takes a long time.

According to researchers patience comes in three main varieties:-

1. Interpersonal patience,
2. Life hardship patience,
3. Daily hassles patience.

Let us look at these in more detail:

1. Interpersonal Patience

Interpersonal patience is patience with other people, their demands and their failings & feelings.

This may considered, some people to be slow learners, hard to understand, or even downright unreasonable. Or, they may have bad habits that may drive us crazy. But losing patience with them will be of no benefit, and it may make matters worse.

Patience and understanding toward others is essential when onboarding new staff, or when delegating tasks. It's also a huge help in dealing with difficult co-workers or managers, and it's central to high-quality customer service.

This type of patience is active. Listening skills and empathy are vital, and, when dealing with difficult people, it needs the self-awareness and emotional intelligence to understand how the words and actions affect the situation. We can't just wait it out and hope for the best.

2. Life Hardship Patience

We could use the term perseverance to sum up life hardship patience. It means having the patience to overcome a serious setback in life, like waiting long term for the outcome of a lawsuit, or for medical treatment. But it can also include your ability to work toward a long-term goal – whether it's professional, such as a promotion, or personal, like getting fit or saving for a vacation.

Whatever the obstacles are to overcome, it will likely require determination and focus to achieve. And it will need to keep emotions under control throughout the journey. These emotions can range from **eagerness to get it done, to anger at the frustrations** we encounter along the way – which can cause us to become demotivated.

3. Daily Hassles Patience

Sometimes we need patience to deal with circumstances that are beyond our control. These are "life hassles." something as trivial as getting stuck in a traffic line, for instance, or waiting for a computer program to load.

We also need patience to get through those dull but unavoidable day-to-day tasks that do not necessarily contribute to personal goals. The ability to maintain self-discipline, and pay the attention up-to the level it needs, is a hallmark of patience.

Medical researchers suggests that people who can stay calm in the face of these constant, petty frustrations are less victim of any mental or physical disorders and are supposed to be more empathic, more equitable, and less affected of depression.

The Benefits and Risks of Patience

In general, being patient means that we are more likely viewed positively by our co-workers and managers (and our family and friends as well). It would be likely a better team player, more focused and productive.

If we are even working hard, but often get impatient, people may see us as arrogant, insensitive and impulsive. Colleagues & co-workers may think that we are a poor decision maker, because we make snap judgments or interrupt people. If we get a reputation for having poor people managing skills and a bad temper, others may even deliberately avoid working with us. As a result, we may lose our reputation and sometimes opportunities to get awarded for the efforts we made by our hard work.

Of course, being patient doesn't mean to be a "pushover." Sometimes it's good or needed to show displeasure when people keep waiting and make delays unnecessarily. So, it has to be ensured that there is an established strong boundary and appropriate target time. But, we should be polite and assertive without being angry and aggressive.

Understanding Impatience

Impatience has its roots in frustration. It's a feeling of rising stress that starts when we feel that our needs & wishes are being ignored. In a modern environment where we're accustomed to instant communication and immediate access to data, it's a growing problem. Understanding the warning signs can help to overcome impatience taking grip.

Impatience Symptoms

Impatience has a range of symptoms. Physical signs can include shallow, fast breathing, muscle tension, hand clenching, and restlessly jiggling feet. There may be changes in mood and thoughts, too. We may become irritable, angry, or experience anxiety or nervousness. Rushing to do things and making snap decisions, the symptoms of hurry sickness appears and impatience is started to gain the upper hand.

Impatience Triggers

If these feelings & symptoms are experienced, we must try to identify the root cause. Many of us have "triggers" for impatience. These could be specific people, words or situations.

We should mark and make a list of things that cause to become impatient. If there is trouble in identifying individuals' triggers, then one should stop and think about the last time when felt this way. What caused it?

Still it is not sure; one should ask your co-workers/ friends/ family members about the cause of impatience. Five whys technique, can also help in identifying the root cause.

It is highly recommended to maintaining a record of feeling impatient along with details of the situation, and root causes of getting frustrated. This can help to examine actions and to understand why the response was in this way. Sometimes, we would not be able to avoid the triggers that make us impatient, but we learn to manage our responses & reactions.

Managing the Symptoms of Impatience

When impatience cast its profound impact, it is very important to overcome the situation and get out of damaging frame of mind as soon as possible. We must develop strategies to deal with our impatience as it is noticed.

Physical Symptoms

The most common and easy recommended steps are to take deep, slow breaths, and count 1-10. Doing this will slow down the heart beat rate, relax the body, and distance emotionally from the situation. Sometimes it might need a longer count, or to repeat the process several times.

Impatience can cause to tense our muscles involuntarily. So, consciously we should focus on relaxing our body . Again, we should take slow, deep breaths and let the muscles from tip top to tip toes be relaxed.

Emotional Symptoms

Habit of thinking positive and challenge negative assumptions are the basic practice to overcome emotional impatience. Aim to reframe the circumstances in a more positive light.

For example, people might not mind if a meeting is delayed and let them know in advance. There might be benefits to the delay: understanding a developing situation more clearly. Telling sorry for delays can bind the people emotionally heart touching experience and overcoming the impact of impatience. Practicing empathy and listening others can also enable us to defuse our impatience.

Case Study: - Once a teacher distributed some confectioneries to the students and all the students were told not to eat for 10 minutes and the teacher came out of the classroom. After 10 minutes, when the teacher came into classroom and checked about the toffees, he found that only 10 % students did not eat, 90% of students did not keep and ate the toffee. The teacher noted down the names of the students who did not eat.

Afterwards, on study, it was found that the students who did not eat the toffee and kept them till further instruction of their teacher, had **higher rate of success in their lives, they achieved more** than those who did not wait for even 10 minutes and ate the toffees.

This activity was done to check the patience. This shows the **degree of patience** and **level of success** is directly proportional to each other.

Highlights

- *Impatience rarely has a positive effect; in fact, it may even interfere with the person's ability to perform.*
- *Impatience will likely generate more conflict and stress, which will be counterproductive.*
- *It would not happen overnight to be more patient, but persistence can overcome resistance.*

Reminders:-

Patience is a vital quality in the workplace.

- Reduces stress and conflicts,
- Leads in better working relationships,
- Helps in achieving long-term career & life goals.
- Supports subordinates to work attentively.

Many of us struggle with impatience. We need to learn to recognize the physical and emotional symptoms associated with it, and to identify the situations that trigger it.

When the causes of impatience are known, we can develop strategies to prevent or overcome it. These could include attending to your physical well-being by using deep breathing and relaxation techniques, and developing our empathy and emotional intelligence skills.

THE 4TH P- PERSISTENCE

(Persistence overcomes resistance)

Persistence is probably one of the most admirable characters a person can possess. It's the ability to be determined to do or achieve something regardless of any setbacks.

When we do something and do not get the desired results, still we continue to doing the things, it is persistence. Persistence is the continuance of effort though it is difficult. **Persistence is the ability to stick with resistances for a long**. Persistence is the quality of continuing work under process steadily confidently. It is the attitude or behaviour a person who continues to do, or try to do, something in a determined way.

A distinguishing attributes of those who succeed in life against those who don't is persistence.

Many people have the capacity to set goals and plans toward success, yet only few succeeds, because only few stick to work on their goals and plans until it is accomplished. Lack of persistence is one of the major causes of failure.

Majority of people stops before they even start properly or they quit in the middle of their journey. Often the reason for quitting is hardships, discomfort and uncertainty. They let their fears and doubts paralyze them from moving persistently toward their goals. Or perhaps, their motivation isn't firm enough to drive them to work on it continuously.

Developing persistence is a master skill to success. It is easier to relax and do nothing, or just live in our comfort zone, rather than face the uncertainty and discomfort of sailing thru our goals. The idea of failure and hardship should be avoided and consistent effort should be made with a will to win. There are mainly **6 ways** to develop the virtue of persistence:-

1. **Identifying Wants and Desires**: - The very first thing is to identify the wants or desires. It can be done by simply writing down specifically all the things to be accomplished. Making lists of all the desires and wants with time target is the key to success, no matter how impossible they are to achieve in the moment.
2. **Motivation**: - Motivation comes from a deep reason with high level of EQ (Emotional quotient) that why we want to achieve or have something. If we know why we are doing what we are doing, it gives more energy to keep moving.
3. **Action plan**: - Identifying wants or desires speaks of **What** to achieve. Determining motivation shows the reasons **Why** to achieve, but outlining definite action steps is to define **How** (methodologies) to achieve. When we know how to get what we want, it makes it easier to achieve it. To know how, it pays to do some research and planning of what needs to be done on our part.
4. **Positive Mental Attitude**: - The road to success is challenging, this is why only few succeeds. There would be countless times to face resistances with scare of failures / defeat and it may be succumbing to negative thoughts of fears and doubts. In order to develop persistence and eventually succeed in our endeavor, always we have to maintain a positive mental attitude, regardless of situation. We should

keep our thoughts focused on taking action towards our goals and avoid negative thoughts and feelings as it may ruin our concentration and persistence.

5. **Mastermind Group**: - Mastermind Group comprises of people who can help us to succeed towards our goal. In choosing we have to be carefully who can be trustworthy and can give unbiased judgments and who has positive mental attitude. We must avoid listening of pessimists.
6. **Discipline and Habit**: - All our goal-setting and planning may go to waste if we won't be able to develop discipline and good habit. Discipline is the bridge between goals and accomplishment. There would be a lot of hindrances that might stop us from moving towards our goal, and without proper discipline, it would be easy to give up in between. Upholding discipline and good habits can help us to stay in the course, even despite difficulties.

It is worth mentioning that setting **smart** goals would be the right approach to develop **consistent persistence** but we have to understand the smart in right sense.

Let us consider the SMART as an abbreviation and let us expand the word a follows:-

S- Specific, M- Measurable, Achievable, R- Realistic, T-Time bond.

We can devise a format as for monitoring the action plan as follows on concept as mentioned above.

What	Why	How	When	Check & Balance	Remarks
Wants/ Desire / Goal	Reasons	Methods	Time target	Weekly monitoring	Remarkable achievements

This format should be displayed at a prominent place in house or office so that this could be before eyes all the time.

Four powers to propel persistence:-

Persistence being a constant effort till the goal is achieved; also needs positive support to keep it up and hence four (4) powers are innovated to propel the process of persistence. The 4 powers are as under:-

1. **POD** (Power of Dream) – This is the most useful tool to stay motivated and stick with the goals. It propels the person to be persistent with high emotional attachments with the goals. Power of dream drives the person to develop an attitude of **will to win – will to work**. The dream is to be determined and put under action plan with 3V approach **Visualize, Verbalize & Vitalize** should be practiced.
2. **POU** (Power of Unity) - This power is all about the collective work in a team spirit approach when the task is performed in a group. Here power of unity propels the people to stick in the group and consistent efforts must ensure persistency.
3. **POS** (Power of Submission) - This power enables to be submitted to the action plan to ensure persistence and goals must be achieved.

4. **POSW** (Power of Spoken Words) – Power of spoken words is the vital tool to propel persistency by speaking repeatedly what we want. This helps to secure mindset so that thought process could support the persistent effort for achieving the goals.

Those who have cultivated the habit of persistence seem to enjoy insurance against failure. No matter how many times they are defeated, they finally arrive up toward the top of the ladder. Sometimes it appears that there is a **hidden Guide** whose duty is to test the people through all sorts of discouraging experiences.

Those who pick themselves up after defeat and keep on trying, arrive, achieve; and the world cries, "Bravo! You did it! We knew you could do it! The hidden Guide lets no one enjoy great achievement without passing the persistence test. Those who cannot take it simply do not make it.

Those who can "take it" are significantly rewarded for their persistence. They receive, as their compensation, whatever goal they are pursuing. That is not all! They receive something infinitely more important than the material compensation-the knowledge that "every failure brings with it the seed of an equivalent advantage."

A River cuts through rock, not because of its power but because of its persistence.

Weakness of persistence:-

The real enemies which stand between we and our noteworthy achievement are the symptoms indicating weakness of persistence. List is as Follows.

1. Failure to recognize and to define clearly exactly what we want.

2. Procrastination, with or without cause.
3. Lack of interest in acquiring specialized knowledge.
4. Indecision, the habit of “passing the buck” on all occasions, instead of facing issues squarely.
5. The habit of relying upon alibis instead of creating definite plans for the solution of problems.
6. Self-satisfaction. The state of being satisfied with what we have, would not motivate to work for more achievement.
7. Indifference, usually reflected in one’s readiness to compromise on all occasions, rather than meets opposition and fights it.
8. The habit of blaming others for one’s mistakes, and accepting unfavorable circumstances as being unavoidable.
9. Weakness of desire, due to neglect in the choice of motives that impel action.
10. Willingness, even eagerness, to quit at the first sign of defeat.
11. Lack of organized plans in writing which may be analyzed when required.
12. The habit of neglecting to move on ideas, or to grasp opportunity when it presents itself.
13. Wishing instead of willing.
14. The habit of compromising with poverty instead of aiming at riches.
15. General absence of ambition ***to be, to do, to own.***
16. Searching for short cuts without giving fair equivalent inputs for the desired outputs. It is usually reflected in the habit of **gambling, endeavoring to drive “sharp” bargains.**

17. Fear of criticism, failure to create plans and put them into action, because of very silly reason that "what people will think".

Highlights:-

- *Persistence defines the degree of determination.*
- *Persistent efforts enhance efficiency & overcome resistances.*
- *Procrastination is the biggest challenges against persistence.*
- *Very long term time target leads to procrastination and tends to failure.*
- *Lack of regular monitoring creates gaps and inconsistency in persistency.*
- ***Ambition is the path** of success but **persistence is the vehicle** to arrive in.*

THE 5TH P- PERFORMANCE

(Performance is the result of persistent practices)

In my personal opinion, when we do something and get the same thing as desired, we are performing. Performance is the conversion of inputs into outputs. The outcome of a process is the same as desired with minimal loss is called good performance.

The accomplishment of a given task measured against preset known standards of accuracy, completeness, cost, and speed. In contractual terms, performance is deemed to be the fulfillment of an obligation, in manner that releases the performer from all liabilities under the contract. Performance is a successful achievement of activities to generate delights for the customers or stake holders.

Performance can be defined as the ability to deliver results based on execution and implementation of set of activities called process.

Performance can be scored & evaluated through following two skills:-

(A) Soft Personal skills – Human beings are born with gifted features by nature and by polishing those features under some experienced guidelines, the person acquires soft skills. Soft skills help a personal in building relationships, gaining better vision, and creating more opportunities for growth & advancement. Seven main soft skills are identified as mentioned below:-

1. Communication

In general practice, utmost importance is given to written and verbal communications. Because they set the tone & text for how people perceive. They also improve the chances of building relationships with people around. **Communication skills boost performance because they help to extract clear expectations from the people so that excellent work could be delivered by them.**

Why employers look for it: Workers are more productive when they know how to communicate with their peers. If we can clearly express **who, what, when, where, why,** and **how** of a project, we would be considered as hot cake.

How to gain it: we can learn and practice to hone our communication and presentation skills under some guidelines of regular training and workshops.

2. Teamwork

Performance is often dependent on team, one person doing something all by him/herself cannot deliver the desired results for an organisation. Success is the result of many people working toward a common goal.

When employees can synthesize their varied talents, everyone wins. That is defined in the following ways considering team as an abbreviation and expanding as hereunder

TEAM →Together Everyone Achieves More.

Employers look to team players to help build a conducive, friendly work culture, which can support retain employees and, in turn attracts top talent. Furthermore, being able to collaborate well with co-workers strengthens the quality of work & better performance.

How to gain it: it needs to generate goodwill amongst people and lend a hand when they are in need. Another way to build rapport is to cover for a colleague while on vacation.

3. Adaptability

Adaptability is a feature converted into skills in a human being to accept and adjust in adverse situations. Things don't always go as planned, and instead of being anguished and distracted, it needs to find an alternate solution. Successful leaders are the ones who know how to be flexible when problems arise. This has deep impact on overall performance and delivering desired results on targeted time.

In the present fast pace of developing scenario, speed of change in any section of life or workplace is rapid, consequently, people need to adapt quick shifts and keep updated with current information so that the performance should be accorded suitably.

How to gain it: it needs to push ourselves to be an early adopter of change. "For example, adapting to technology without thinking much about the past, no matter how tougher it is for people who are used to perform in the existing practices, someone who is capable of meeting new challenges should go ahead, should arrange for the training sessions and offer to teach them.

4. Problem solving

When something goes wrong, we can either complain or take action. Action means corrective preventive actions with an action plan that would be a positive step towards performance and would be noticed. It would make a person indispensable performer.

Society, industries, companies all over in the world, people rely on problem solvers and they are considered as top performers and supposed to navigate unexpected challenges.

To develop this skill, we should always approach to our experienced seniors with some suggestions having solutions. The brain storming sessions with 5Why analysis is highly recommended for the root cause finding and could CAPA (Corrective Action & Preventive Action).

5. Critical observation

Critical observation of data means the interpretation of data to know the facts and proficiency of outcome. Through critical observation we can help in understanding the actual status and potential scope of improvements in the process. A critical observation can help to make a better worker all around.

Growing companies / organisations always need critical analyzers/ thinkers who bring a fresh perspective and offer intuitive solutions and ideas to help the company / organisation get a leg up on the competition or improve internal processes.

To be a critical observer, we need to be able to analyze information and put it to use. One tactic is to try to identify patterns of behavior at work. For example, we should note the reactions on weekly sales reports during the weekly MRM. Negative reactions are more significant to note down for CAPA (Corrective Actions & Preventive Actions). By observing how people respond to the constant flow of information we can better understand the critical aspects of improving business operations.

6. Conflict resolution

When more than one person into an organization are put for an assignment, there is going to be some conflicts, "its human nature." Therefore, being able to resolve issues becomes imperative to maintain relationships with peers and work more effectively.

Capability of working constructively through disagreements with people is a sure indicator of maturity and leadership potential as well. This would help to promote a healthy, collaborative workplace.

The best way to resolve disagreements between co-workers is to address issues directly but delicately in a judgment-free environment and then working together to find a solution.

7. Leadership

Leadership skills having confidence and a clear vision can help in influencing team and get them on board with our ideas now and in the future. Such leadership skills help to have good vision of growth within an organization, which can lead to more opportunities for both personal performance and organizational growth.

Organisations / companies are always looking for employees with leadership potential because those workers will one day be taking over the reins and building on the company's legacy. In spite of getting people to do what we want, Leadership means inspiring and helping others to reach their full potential which gives the opportunity to manage people, learn how to motivate a team, and take on more responsibility.

(B) Professional Hard skills- Hard skills include the specific knowledge and abilities required for success by learning through formal education and on job practical training.

Examples of hard skills include computer programming, web design, typing, accounting, finance, writing, and mathematics, legal and other quantifiable skills that are included in the requirements for a job in organisations / institutions.

Hard skills are part of the skill set that is required for a job. They include the expertise necessary for an individual to perform the job. They are job-specific and are typically listed in job postings and job descriptions.

Hard skills are acquired through formal education and training programs, including college, apprenticeships, short-term training classes, online courses, certification programs, as well as by on-the-job training.

To ensure better performance, both hard skills and soft skills are important in the workplace. Organisations are always seeking people having hard skills with good soft skills as well. Soft skills that enable to perform in managing the activities, the hard skills ensure in delivering the specific assignments.

Performance management

Performance management can be defined as an ongoing process of communication between management and its employees of an organisation in support of accomplishing the strategic objectives including clarifying expectations, setting objectives, identifying goals, providing feedback, and reviewing results at regular intervals.

Overseeing performance and providing feedback is not an event to be focused in an annual performance review. It is an ongoing process that takes place throughout the year at an interval of defined period in process and people as well. Performance management is a process of ensuring that the set of activities and outputs meet an **organization's goals** in an effective and efficient manner. Performance management can focus on the **performance of an entire organization, a department, an employee, or the processes in place** to manage particular tasks.

The Performance Management process is a cycle, with discussions varying year-to-year based on changing objectives. The cycle includes Planning, Checking-In, and Review periodically. It is widely known as PDCA (Plan Do Check Act) cycle also.

To start planning process for the set performance period, management first discusses the existing status, past reviews and explains overall expectations which include collaborating on the development of **performance objectives.** Individual development goals are also updated. Then a performance plan is devised that directs the employee's efforts toward achieving specific results to support organizational excellence along with employee performance. Goals and objectives are discussed throughout the year; during MRM (Management Review Meetings).

At the end of the performance period, management reviews employee's **performance against expected objectives, as well as the means used and behaviors demonstrated in achieving those objectives** then after management discuss and establishes **new objectives** for the next performance period.

Performance Evaluation:

Performance Evaluation is defined as a formal and productive procedure to measure an employee's work and results based on their job responsibilities. It is used to gauge the amount of value added by an employee in terms of increased business revenue, in comparison to industry standards and overall employee return on investment (ROI).

All organizations that have learned the art of **"winning from within"** by focusing on their people's involvements and participation to rely on a systematic **performance evaluation** process to measure and evaluate their performance on regular basis. Ideally, employees are graded annually on their work anniversaries on the basis of which, they are either promoted or suitable recognition in terms of salary hikes. Performance evaluation also plays a direct role in providing periodic feedback to employees, such that they are more self-aware in terms of their own performance metrics.

Objectives of Performance Evaluation.

- Periodic performance evaluation is report card of individuals as well as management / organisation that acknowledges the work done in a specific time period and after analysis we can find the scope for betterment and further improvement.
- An organisation can provide consistent feedback on an employee's strengths and strive for improvement in the areas that the employees need to work on.
- It is an integral platform for both, the employee and employer, to attain a common ground on what both think is befitting a **Quality performance**. This helps in improving communication which usually leads to better and more accurate team metrics and thus, **improved performance results**.

- The goal of this entire process of performance evaluation is to improve the way a team or organization functions, to achieve **higher levels of customer satisfaction**.
- Management should evaluate their team member on regular intervals and not just once a year. This way, the team can avert new and unexpected problems with constant work being done to improve **competence and efficiency**.
- An organization's management can conduct frequent employee's training and skill development sessions on the basis of the areas recognized for the development after a **performance evaluation session.**
- Regular performance evaluation can help determine the scope of growth in an employee's career and the level of motivation with which he / she contributes towards the success of an organization.
- Further, management can effectively manage the team and conduct productive resource allocation after evaluating the goals and preset standards of performance.
- Performance evaluation lets an employee understand where he / she stand as compared to others in the organization.

Performance Evaluation Methods

There are 5 most critical performance evaluation methods.

Using only one of these performance evaluation methods might help an organization merely gain one-sided information, while, using multiple of these methods help in obtaining insights from various perspectives which will be instrumental in forming an unbiased and performance-centric decision.

1. **Self-Evaluation**: This is an amazing method to get started with employee reviews. Self-evaluation is when an employee is expected to rate themselves using multiple-choice or open-ended questions, by keeping in mind some evaluation criteria. After conducting self-evaluation, the management has an opportunity to fairly assess an employee by considering his/her thoughts about their performance.
2. **360-degree Employee Evaluation**: In this performance evaluation method, an employee is a rated in terms of the advancements made by him/her within the team as well as with external teams. Inputs from supervisors of different departments are considered along with evaluation done by direct supervisors and immediate peers too. Thus, in 360 degree feedback, each employee is rated for the job done according to their job description as well the work done by them in association with other teams.
3. **Graphics Rating Scale**: This is one of the most widely used performance evaluation methods by supervisors. Numeric or text values corresponding to values from poor to excellent can be used in this scale and parallel evaluation of multiple team members can be conducted using this graphical scale. Employee skills, expertise, conduct and other qualities, in comparison to others in a team, can be evaluated. It is important to make each employee understand the value of each entity of the scale in terms of success and failure. This scale should ideally be the same to each employee.

4. **Developmental Checklists**: Every organization has a certain roadmap for each employee for their developments as well as exhibited behavior. This method of maintaining a checklist for development is one of the most straightforward performance evaluation methods. This checklist has several dichotomous questions, answers of which need to be positive. If not, then the employee requires some developmental training in the areas where he/she needs improvement.
5. **Demanding Events Checklist**: There are events in each employee's career with an organization where he/she has to exhibit immense skill and expertise. An intelligent manager always tends to keep a demanding events list where employees show good or bad qualities.

To have an impactful performance evaluation, we must coordinate it in the most professional manner by making sure the negatives do not overpower the positives. This is a testimony to the manager's leadership skills as well as the employee's yearly performance.

Some Effective Questions for performance evaluation:-

1. What motivates you to get your job done well?
2. Which tasks do you enjoy doing the most?
3. Which tasks you don't enjoy at all and why?
4. What are the 3 things as an organization we can do better?
5. On a scale of 0-10, how likely are you to refer us to your family or friends?

Survey Questions for Effective Leadership

1. Do you feel the leadership in this organization treats everyone fairly?
2. What leadership qualities do you associate yourself with?
3. Can you give us an example or an incident where you used leadership traits in this organization?
4. Do you think there is effective communication between employees and leadership in this organization?
5. If you are replaced with one of the leaders in this organization what advice would you give the employees?

Survey Questions for Value Addition

1. What are the things you have done to improve the overall success of this organization?
2. What is your idea of recognition?
3. Do you receive regular feedback from your peers/manager/supervisor?
4. How many sensitive projects have you handled in your association with the organization?
5. Do you feel valued in this organization?

Survey Questions for Workplace Culture

1. Have you proposed any effective changes in office policies or procedures?
2. How often do you communicate with your manager/peers?
3. Do you help your peers with the information they need to successfully complete their tasks?

4. Have you had any unpleasant discussion with your team members/manager/ supervisor?
5. How do you think you can bring about a positive change in the workplace culture?

Performance Evaluation Steps:-

Step 1: In most organizations, a performance evaluation process states that an employee's performance is tracked every three and six months, provided, the employee has worked with the organization continually for that tenure. The HR department can send across an online survey for the employees to fill out regarding their satisfaction and engagement levels.

Step 2: The employee's immediate manager will decide his/her performance quality after evaluating the yearly performance, conducting an employee engagement survey and eventually having a face-to-face meeting.

Step 3: The feedback received from the online employee satisfaction survey can be kept anonymous. This feedback can be analyzed in real-time from a centralized dashboard. On the basis of the analysis, the manager can prepare further questions for the face-to-face performance evaluation meeting.

For a probationary employee to be termed as a tenured employee, he/she must perform as per their supervisor's expectations for six months. The first six months of an employee's tenure are crucial as the management always has a watchful eye on them for all their contribution towards assigned tasks, ownership skills and punctuality in task completion.

After confirmation, an immediate manager will evaluate the non-probationary employee on a yearly basis.

Tips to have a smooth Performance Evaluation Process

- The supervisor should avoid being too negative or positive with the employees
- Should express displeasure in the most positive manner possible.
- He/she should communicate with the employee prior to the review meeting about preparing any questions they might have for the supervisor.
- It is highly recommended for a manager to prepare a list of general topics to discuss with the team member, as an evaluation discussion is ideal for all topics which remain un-discussed throughout the year.
- Every manager must communicate the employee's future plans with the organization in the performance evaluation meeting.
- The supervisor should always end the evaluation process on a positive note.

Process performance:-

Evaluation of process performance is done by evaluating capability of process.

Capability of process means the process parameters are robust enough to convert inputs into results as desired and are well defined in a well devised SOP (Standard operating procedure).

Technically, performance can be understood through the following mathematical formula **Output = Inputs X Process.**

Output is measured in percentage and is called performance. High percentage of performance is dependent of **CP** (Capability of Process).

Capability of process means the process parameters are robust enough to convert inputs into results as desired and are well defined in a well devised SOP (Standard operating procedure).

Capability of process is determined through mathematical calculation based on practical study of repeatability and reproducibility considering a sample size calculated the process is considered capable of delivering desired required results in terms of quality products (Details calculation formula can be discussed and demonstrated while personal consultancy by the author on demand)

Performance vs. Success: - Performance is a part of success. Success is a lifetime long journey and performance is a small stopover to start next assignment after completion of the task in hand.

We all have our own definition of success. For many of us it's measured primarily in terms of money and wealth, but there are clearly other important aspects of success.

Some people value the freedom to spend their time as they want; others value the ability to help those in need. Yet, whatever the metric, there are a core set of personality traits that are common to all successful people.

Five Traits of Successful People: - Attaining success is not simply a matter of luck. It's a matter of making efforts and taking the time to learn a trade, applying your knowledge and sticking with it even in the face of adversity and potential failure along the way.

While successful people come in all shapes and sizes and work in many different fields, they tend to share key character traits which help them get and stay ahead.

Here are five traits of successful people. By cultivating these traits and making them part of daily habits would lead to success in life and career as well.

1. **Aspiration-** Successful people have clear-cut goals. Instead of vague goals like "become rich," their goals will be specific, like "expand from one to three stores within the next two years." **SMART** (**S**pecific, **M**easurable, **A**chievable, **R**ealistic, **T**ime bond) goals are the key to sure success.

   By gaining clarity on the goals, it makes them more possible to attain. First, the goals become specific motivating factors that keep going when times get tough. Second, these goals provide a blueprint for their career. They have something specific to work toward. With their idea of success is defined, they can break down the goals into more manageable milestones which can be worked toward incrementally.

2. **Determination drive- O**ne of the most defining traits of successful people is their determination drive. After all, setting clear goals is one thing. However, successful people must have a strong drive to actually attain their goals. It's that so-called "**fire in the belly**" that motivates them to succeed. It gives them a laser focus so that they can devote all of their attention and efforts toward furthering their progress toward their dreams. A successful person must have **aptitude** with a strong sense of drive is able to work tirelessly, because they believe in their abilities and truly want to attain their goals.

3. **Willingness to learn-** One of the most important traits of successful people is a genuine desire and willingness to learn. Successful people always keep their mind open. They try to learn from everyone and every situation they come across. Every experience offers an opportunity to grow.

   They can admit when they don't know something...and will be motivated to improve their knowledge when they realize they have room to learn something new. This receptivity keeps their minds alert. Lifelong learning means that they are constantly exposed to new ideas and inspirations.

4. **Patience-** Patience is a virtue, which enables to withstand even in adverse situations and ultimately reach to success. It is not the most exciting trait, it's invaluable. As much as we all want things to happen right now, success takes time. **Anything that is worth attaining is worth waiting for.**

People who are bound to achieve great things recognize this, and they're willing to take it slow but steady to win the race. Patience allows them to persist even in the face of adversity because they have the foresight to learn from mistakes and see that they will pay off in the future. Being patient isn't always fun. It can be challenging. But in the long run, it would be rewarding with longevity and steadiness in the career if we can cultivate the trait of patience.

5. **Discipline-** Success rewards consistency. To be consistent, you have to have discipline. Working hard for a week and then slacking off isn't going to yield incredible results. Many of the most successful people find that **establishing a routine is one of the keys to making their dreams a reality**, as it allows them to be consistent in their efforts.

Everyone's routine will be a little different; it will vary from individual to individual. However, some common routines of successful people might involve waking up early to get everyday tasks out of the way and filter through emails before the workday begins, or taking 30 minutes to read each day to increase their knowledge base and prowess (skills) in their chosen field. By being consistent and disciplined and devoting to grow, we can reap many rewards in work and in life. This is a key trait that allows people to enjoy not only success but longevity in their career.

An action plan based on PDCA approach along-with clearly defined Why, What, When, How would be the right way to get desired success. This is already described in the previous chapter in details.

It is probably true that the success of one's life depends on factors outside of one's control. If so, then no one can have a duty to lead a good life. Still, **excluding the effects of luck**, we can say that each human being will have a more or less successful life **depending on the decisions they make and the options they pursue.** And we can add that each human being has a comprehensive duty to lead a successful life, to the extent that it is within his or her power to do so.

Highlights

- *Performance means the fulfillment of tasks to create desired required results.*
- *Performance is a result of planned and persistent effort.*
- *Performance is a combination of personal & professional outcomes.*
- *SMART planning with TEAM spirit produces good performance.*
- *Persistent performance leads to consistent growth.*
- *Performance does depend on luck when luck is considered as an abbreviation (LUCK) and expanded as **L**earning **U**nder **C**orrect **K**nowledge.*

THE 6TH P- PROSPERITY

(Everyone is the Secret to their own Prosperity)

In my opinion, **Prosperity** can be defined as the state of living an ***Enjoyable Pleasant peaceful & purposeful life*** in all respect in all aspects of life. Prosperity in true sense that is **prosperity in totality** leads to a **Perfect life.** Prosperity is not to overcome poverty, but to change the status of living and it is a continual process. Prosperity and poverty both are the state of living; the difference is how the life is enjoyed.

Let us consider the **six (6) states of living conditions** and their consequences:-

S.N	State of living condition	Consequences	Remarks
1	Having everything as per need / want but do not have time to enjoy.	Wealth prosperity, but time poverty.	Temporary happiness. Busy life.
2	Having enough time to enjoy but lack of so many things what is needed / wanted.	Time prosperity but wealth poverty.	No happiness, Life in crisis.
3	Having things in abundance what is waned / needed and time also to enjoy them but cannot enjoy due to ill physical conditions.	Wealth & time prosperity but Health poverty.	No happiness, Life in distress.

4	Having Time, wealth and health in balance but less recognition in social life or bad relationship with people.	Prosperity with poor relationship amongst people.	Happy animal life. Not human life.
5	Having Time, wealth, health and good social recognition, but lack of spiritual emotions and feelings.	Prosperity with poor spirituality.	Happy human life limited to selfishness.
6	Having enough Time, wealth, health, recognition with full of spiritualism and usefulness for the **Humanity.**	Enjoyable pleasant purposeful life.	Life with Prosperity & sweet contentment. **Perfect life**.

Prosperity and poverty both are relative terms and always vary according to situation, circumstances and comparison. Prosperity is not overcoming poverty but to convert present lifestyle and thought process to generate pleasure and contentment. It is an everlasting process and never ending practices to enjoy the essence of life.

Normally having wealth & riches in terms of property, gold, money are considered prosperity but in my views, the self-defined and well versed matrix of living conditions as per above chart, clearly shows that the last (6th) one is the best one and the prosperity in real sense exists here that is **prosperity in totality**.

Creating physical wealth in right ways and utilizing them appropriately for the right purpose would always be appreciated for a prosperous life.

It is worth mentioning that physical wealth & riches are subject to be consumed, utilized, wasted or taken away by others in due periods of time , but the prosperity remains and multiplies if the wealth & riches are appropriately utilized in creating joys and fulfillment of needs and positive dreams that may support society and overall human beings. The enjoyable pleasant & purposeful life is not met only in earning wealth & riches but to utilize them in right purpose.

But for being useful or doing useful deeds, we must have all wanted / desired things in abundance with contentment and saturation.

We think sometimes that poverty is only being **hungry, naked and homeless,** but the poverty of being **unwanted, unloved and uncared** might be the **greatest poverty** and the efforts made towards overcoming these situations could be **the right prosperity** which in turn ensures **enjoyable pleasant peaceful & purposeful life.**

Human life is formed by the perspectives and philosophies adapted. Changing the perspectives can create an immediate shift in life and business as well. To succeed as an Entrepreneur we must constantly look for ways to sharpen our perspectives.

It is established fact that we **get paid for bringing values** to the marketplace, and if we are not very valuable or unable to generate values, we are unable to make much money and physical wealth or riches. If we understand this powerful philosophy and implement it into our life, **we would develop a substantial advantage over those who don't.**

Most of the people often blame the economy, their job or the government for their lack of income, but they don't make much effort to improve their values or skills. **The harsh reality we all must understand is we would always be paid exactly what we are worth, or we must expect what we are worthy of.**

If somebody is making minimum wage, that's the value they're bringing to the market place. Why does somebody make Rs.1000/- an hour while many others make Rs.100/- an hour? It's quite simple. One has become more valuable to the marketplace than the others.

When we generate more values to the marketplace, we create more wealth. As an entrepreneur, we must consistently find ways to become more valuable. The quicker we understand this, faster we can advance in our fast paced economy and prosperity so generated would be contemporarily utilized for the betterment and improvement of society.

Time on a job, years at a specific occupation, does not increase the **inherent value** of the job being done or, in many cases after the first few years, the value of the employee, either.

We often hear people say **"I have more than 20 years of experience, I should be paid more." but, in fact , that person has one year of experience repeated 20 times**, why would they expect more money? They aren't becoming more valuable unless they're sharpening their skills, learning better tools and constantly trying to make themselves better.

It is Value that guarantees a higher income, age doesn't. We cannot get more valuable hanging around for years. **Age is not value**. People, who want more money, must earn by delivering more values to the business and customers.

As entrepreneurs, we have the ability to create much more income as long as we understand this concept of value addition.

Things to focus on: - We must learn to work harder on ourselves than we do on our job. If we work hard on our job we make a living, but if **we work hard on ourselves** we would make ourselves an asset and create **prosperity in totality.**

To generate prosperity, we don't need to go to work on the economy; we don't need to change our company, the government, our bosses or often our circumstances. We need to go to work on ourselves. **When we change, everything changes for us**. If we remain constant, and we change companies, tactics, strategies or mentors, we would still be the constant and no value addition would take place in ourselves. Striving for becoming a better person **ensures better prosperity**, Instead of comparing and differentiating with others. The only person we need to change and bring betterment is to make change in us and find ourselves different than we were yesterday.

How to create 'value' to the marketplace: - By becoming better in all respect in all aspects, we would quickly advance in the game of economics when we consistently build our character, skills and value to others.

Physical Prosperity could be ensured by making growth as an integral part of daily agenda, and doing something that increases the value we bring to our business, our work, our clients or customers. It is not very complicated to change our current income and increase prosperity level. We simply need to offer more values to the marketplace.

1. To enhance **prosperity quotient**, here are some areas where we can reliably find opportunities to increase our **values** and stand out against the competitions.
2. **Expertise →** Enhancing skills & competence.
3. **Productivity→** Increasing outputs with respect to inputs.
4. **Efficiency→** High rate of input conversion methods.
5. **Organization / multiplication→** Less manual labor, more automation.
6. **Influence→** Guide & follow-up
7. **Celebrity status→**Degree of recognition amongst target audience / customers
8. **Reputation→** How good /bad people think about us or organisation/ work **p**lace.
9. **Vision→**To see & think different what others do not & have long term action plan.
10. **Personality→**How well we connect and treat / deal with the people.
11. **Attitude→** Thought & Action towards self and others.
12. **Awareness→**Knowing our strengths and what we are the best at.
13. **Masterminding→** Association with people we can learn from.

There are unlimited infinite ways to achieve success and convert the success into prosperity. As an entrepreneur when we commit to grow to a higher level, always there is the greatest time for those who make the decision not to tolerate mediocrity, and take full (100%) responsibility for their **economic wellbeing** that is physical prosperity. Commitment to become more **valuable, we can** always be in control of our economy regardless of outside circumstances and can create prosperity in totality.

PRINCIPLES OF PROSPERITY

A) Spiritual (Metaphysical) principles of prosperity

1. **Law of rebound→** it is supposed that wealth & happiness comes most easily to those who forget the self in the service to others. The law of giving infallibly returns more to the giver than what they contribute.
2. When we focus on other people and circumstances as the source of our prosperity, we tend to lose it, but when we recognize God, a Higher Power or 'the Universe' as the source of our supply, money begins to flow
3. Our job, employer, investments or spouse seem to be the source of our money, but these are just 'externals' that mask the metaphysical sources of abundance. Actual money does not make us secure; what does is a thorough knowledge of the universe's power to provide.
4. To receive our 'good', we must first cleanse our mind of clutter and negative emotions. In forming a vacuum, we allow good things to rush in. When we hold in resentment, we are bound to that person or situation that we resent. In forgiving, we free ourselves and allow the **floodgates of prosperity** to open.
5. The universe is perfectly ordered, therefore the person who makes their own affairs more orderly is attuned to universal riches. To receive more money, we must first demonstrate that we can manage well what we have now, however little.

6. **The basic law of the universe** is that things come into being which did not exist before. When we create **mental pictures of health, wealth and happiness**, we are not trying to change the laws of nature, but instead fulfilling our unique promise to bring these things into being.

7. **According to the law of attraction**, whatever we put our attention on thought or desire, it becomes reality. We attract to ourselves things or people that are the equivalent of our current state of being, or 'vibration'.

8. **The 'creative process'** is the specific way we can use the law of attraction to obtain what we want. It involves: Asking the universe, and being very clear about what we want; Believing, acting and speaking as though we have already received what we have asked for; and Receiving – feeling great that it is coming to us, which sets up the necessary vibration to manifest the desire. The principle works on the basics that **WHATEVER MIND OF A MAN CAN CONCEIVE AND BELIEVE, IT CAN ACHIEVE.**

   Deciding to elevate our mood or feeling in each moment is vital for increasing our vibration, which in turn attracts things, people and feelings of a like vibration. To be both rich and happy, we must make a **positive mental attitude** a basic habit of living.

9. Gratitude is the key to an abundant life, because it puts us in a state of mind that attracts even more of what we are grateful for. **Love, appreciation and thanks are the essence of prosperity**. It is right to become a giver, but we must also learn to be good receivers as well.

B) Wealth creation principles of Prosperity.

1. The foundation of a prosperous life (combining material wealth, health and mental wellbeing) is personal character, formed from self-control and cultivation of virtues. A person of integrity, trust and good character is 'bankable'; their riches evolve out of who they are as much as what they do.
2. Well defined, determined & definite purpose is basic essential element of the success in the process of wealth creation. A clear purpose enables us to see setbacks as temporary, banishes fear and doubt, and inspires others to support in the process.
3. Whatever we do, provide or create, make sure we do it in an outstanding way putting our bests. Doing a little more than is asked or expected or **'going the extra mile'** by putting in an extraordinary effort with no fear of loss is the basis of creating great fortunes.
4. The fear of failure or embarrassment is the **greatest obstacle** in achieving wealth. **Fear puts a brake on action**, yet if we are not willing to fail we will forever be bound in circumstances that involve little risk. **With little risk there are only small rewards.**
5. **Principle of Learn, don't blame**. It is easy to blame people or events when things are not going smooth, but the **enlightened wealth creator** seeks only to learn in every situation. We should never **complain but, look for opportunities.**
6. **Thinking big** is the basis of all great enterprises and fortunes. We are constantly thinking, therefore it takes no more effort to think big instead of small. Thinking out of box is the key.

7. Wealth flows to the person who has a high toleration for uncertainty or disappointment. Handling disappointments properly, will enable to make more attempts to achieve the goals.
8. Law of averages says, where others have given up the struggler will succeed. Wealth-minded people do not try to avoid risk or complexity. They even embrace large problems because they know that solving them can produce great value.
9. It is not enough to want to be rich, we must commit to it. Providence moves all for the person who determines to stick it out, doing that they can to make a venture work. **The half-hearted achieve half-success or failure.** The seed of entrepreneurship is a wish to be in control of our own destiny.
10. If we think we see the future, we must act on it. Hunches based on in-depth knowledge are usually right. If something captures our imagination, chances are it will capture that of others too.
11. Everything that we see around us, someone has made a fortune from it. All we need is one idea that can make us to create our fortune, and it is probably to be found in our own thought.
12. One must not be afraid to be different. On entering any new field or an industry, one should aim to really shake it up and provide new value. The surest way to wealth is to create a product or service that increases the ease and speed of results.
13. Above all, it is customers that create wealth. Have customers before we even start our business.
14. The purpose of entrepreneurship is to deliver new satisfaction and value. It is built on 'unexpected successes' that are quickly capitalized upon.

15. Having many sources of income provides financial security. Wealthy people create many money-producing systems. Middle class people work within the system or for these systems, and so never get rich
16. All wealth is created first in the mind then thought & innovative actions create prosperity.

C) Wealth management principles of prosperity.

1. We should live within our means. If we are not wealthy, do not have a wealthy lifestyle. We will get rich by imitating the mindsets of the wealthy, not by imitating their spending.
2. Poor people are focused on **spending money**; the wealthy people are focused on **creating it, saving it and investing it**.
3. Most people see money as cash in their hands to be used and spent. Wealthy people understand money primarily as seeds to be planted that will grow into money trees.
4. We should plan our spending. We should never shop on impulse. The longer we plan a purchase, generally the more money we will save.
5. We should document our spending. We must write down everything we spend. It is the first step in getting control of our finances.
6. We should become a habitual saver. We should pay ourselves the first ten per cent of what we earn, before tax, and invest it. The discipline of saving (given a certain amount of time) can make us rich. We must not risk our peace of mind or relationships by chasing the quick money.

7. We should save money through using the magic of compound interest by reinvesting all interest or dividends earned. Savings allow us to pick up bargains and take advantage of opportunities.
8. Earning more is good but will not solve our debt problem (debts increase to match earnings). Learning how to manage money responsibly will solve the debt problem.
9. The **frugal** (**Mitavyayee**) people who optimize their expenses **enjoy** what they have more, **get** more use out of what they own, and **get delighted** in the ability to make gifts when they wish.
10. We should have a **contingency plan** under our saving plans to have an **emergency fund** that can cover our living expenses for about six months. If something happens, we will not have to go into debt or depend on the charity of others.
11. We should avoid more uses of credit cards. Debit cards now perform all the functions that credit cards were once useful for, and will not lead us into a debt spiral. If we practice to pay for most of the things with cash, we will spend less.
12. When borrowing money, we should make sure that it is for a productive asset or one that is likely to appreciate, and we should pay off the loan as soon as possible.
13. Being someone who 'knows the price of everything and the value of nothing' cannot create worth, in stock investing; one should consider himself a part owner of a company, not a trader.
14. One should not try to beat the market or speculate. One should trust the long term ability of stock markets to overall deliver good returns.

15. Using the power of leverage and modest price appreciation, plus a normal degree of patience, in two or three decades one can build a real estate fortune.
16. Too little or too much money **magnifies personal deficiencies, or reveals the good character** that was already there. Therefore, in relation to our financial life, we should take care of our personal qualities are never wasted.

D) Sharing and circulation principles of Prosperity.

1. Money is a kind of energy, always active. To bring the greatest benefit to the greatest number, it must flow and circulate.
2 Generating, using and spending money in a way that is consistent with our deepest values has a healing effect not only on us, but also the world.
3. We never really possess wealth, but are stewards of it until we die. When a fortune is made, the creator has a duty to apply at least some of it to causes and projects that will assist and elevate others. With clear goals and a focus on results, **private wealth in the form of foundations can change the world.**
4. Prosperity's foundation is a healthy natural environment. Without clean air, water and a fertile earth we have nothing. One should invest, spend or make money in a way that causes no harm and is good for the planet. If given access to finance, the world's poorest people will strive for, and achieve, self-reliance and prosperity.

Highlights

- *Prosperity can be defined as the state of living an Enjoyable Pleasant peaceful & purposeful life.*
- *Prosperity is not to overcome poverty, but to change the status of living.*
- *Prosperity is not overcoming poverty but to convert present lifestyle and thought process to generate pleasure and contentment.*
- *It is Value that guarantees a higher income, age doesn't.*
- *People, who want more money, must earn by delivering more values.*
- *Striving for becoming a better person ensures better prosperity.*
- *Love, appreciation and thanks are the essence of prosperity.*
- *The fear of failure is the greatest obstacle; it puts a brake on action.*

THE 7TH P- PERFECTION

(Perfection is the result of Persistent Practices)

Perfection is a state of quality of the highest degree of proficiency and skill that meets the feature of the highest degree of excellence. Perfection means free of all defects. Perfection means nothing less than what it should be.

Perfection is the outcome of **defect free performances** by **defect free inputs** while converted through **defect free processes.**

Anything having its **highest level of attainment is perfection**. When we get the things exactly what was planned to get in the same magnitude and required desired quality as we thought is the perfection in that point of time for that attainment.

Perfection is beyond correction but if there is a scope of correction, then it is not perfection. Perfection is a destination to go through the small steps of performances and subsequent gradual successes. It is a goal to achieve and needs consistent persistent practices.

Perfection in human life is all about the perfect alignment of Physique, Mind and Soul. It is the condition of human life from what is possible for the human to achieve, beyond the merely acceptable, the adequate and the best we can do in the given circumstances. In my view, perfection should be defined actively, not nominally.

In other words, **perfection is an action, an activity, a pursuit, not a thing or static state**. With practice, a swimmer perfects her stroke and a golfer perfects his swing.

And to what end is this practice directed? In my view, it is directed toward the attainment of some ideal state. Both the swimmer and the golfer have in mind an image of an ideal stroke or swing which they strive to replicate or achieve with repetition and dedication.

Attaining this ideal state is not easy. It requires diligence and discipline, leading to only rare moments when the ideal is truly met, or may be more accurately – fleeting glimpsed. Instead, more realistically, what the golfer and swimmer achieve is a good habit. Their hard work and practice produce a highly **effective consistency in performance**, punctuated by rare moments of near-perfection. But no matter how skillful one becomes, the ideal state is always just beyond reach and the perfection is to achieve the same.

Now if we consider **perfection of human life** as it is with swimming, golf, etc. so it is with life also. Perfection is not limited to isolated physical skills. Mental skills, attitudes, emotions, dispositions, etc. all can be perfected in various ways.

Life is a skill, and that skill can be practiced and improved, and that improvement can be aimed at an ideal condition.

The skills of life can become habitually effective and can at times produce ephemeral (temporary) encounters with true perfection – moments of transcendence when we experience the indescribable sense of having touched an ideal state.

Ideal state is a state of any thoughts, objects, processes, results, achievements and attainments when perfection meets its highest order of performance, but the condition of being ideal might be different for every thought, object, process, result, achievement and attainment.

The state is again not stable as defined or assumed because of personal capabilities of each individual in terms of **vision, value, volume, and velocity to perform.**

In other words, when we consider perfection in **material things or objects**, we find variations in defining perfections depending on various affecting factors for different views of people in the form of shape, size, dimension, color, look, appearance, attachment & appurtenant and hence perfection as an absolute perfection cannot be defined well for all in general. It may be considered in a particular state of presence and situation of any object or material things for a certain purpose of utilization and intended desired results, otherwise, it might be setting limits for further innovations & improvements. In the materialistic point of view, when perfection is considered as a thought and realization of the thoughts in the form of objects, in that point of time, we see the things perfect subject to change again anytime through new thoughts, new innovations and new definitions.

Hence, **perfection is never an end point, it is always an idea of getting more and better things** through enhancing knowledge based on regular new experiences through new surroundings, new phenomenon, new incidences and happenings.

All Human beings have three state of knowledge level as described hereunder.

1. **We know what we know (WKWWK)**

This state defines and signifies our actual acquired level of subjective or professional knowledge, expertise, education, experience etc. and the **perfection** of performance is accorded as per the capability & capacity built on the skill and competence acquired through the level of knowledge, expertise, education, experience.

2. **We know what we do not know (WKWWDNK)**

This state defines and signifies about our knowledge of things we do not have. We know that we do not have any subjective knowledge, expertise, experience, education etc. on certain subjects or professions. Here, we try to know more as and when need may be under prevailing circumstances and enhance our capabilities but the **perfection** of performance is seized accordingly.

3. **We do not know what we do not know (WDNKWWDNK)**

This is the state of being empty & blank about the things exists but do not have any idea that further what is left to know or even what are the things else to know till they appear. Under these circumstances, we have to have learning aptitude with an attitude of adaptability for new things and change of mindset.

Level of **Perfection** of performance varies according to above three states and hence perfection is always a contemporary level of achievements not an absolute thing. Therefore, it can be concluded that the perfection is a nonexistent thing; it is only an idea of ideal thoughts. Yet, the common adage (proverb) that "**no one is perfect, nothing is perfect**" seems to suggest that perfection is an unrealistic and unattainable goal but to make continuous effort for an ideal state.

Perfectionism & Excellence

Perfectionism is pursuing the best possible human life with excellence, ethics or politics that prioritize goals of good living as described hereunder:

- **A theory of values in which a "**good life" means one aimed at the highest "good," either for oneself, or for the world in general, where "good" may be defined differently by different philosophers. However, all perfectionist philosophies assume some objective notion of the "good"—not whatever you feel like or desire.
- **As a theory of ethics**, that perfectionism, as defined above, determines what is morally right and wrong; in other words, whatever serves the highest "good" is morally right.
- **A theory in which political systems and government** policies should serve the perfectionist agenda; in other words, that politics should create the conditions for attaining the highest "good" for either individuals or humanity as a whole.

These philosophies are separable but cumulative. We can easily be a philosophical perfectionist without being an ethical or political perfectionist, but not the other way around; ethical and political perfectionism assume value-perfectionism. And, historically, philosophers often combine all three positions.

Many famous philosophers have been perfectionists—such as Aristotle, Aquinas, Spinoza, and Marx.

Societies around the world today seem to assume philosophical perfectionism; it is normal to assume that **self-improvement, professional accomplishment, and changing the world for the better are the purposes of life.**

Perfectionism may be defined as a moral theory directs human beings to protect and promote objectively good human lives.

In **ethics** and value theory, **perfectionism** is the persistence of will in obtaining the optimal quality of **spiritual, mental, physical, and material being**.

In other words, **perfectionism** can be described as an account of the good life, or the intrinsically desirable life.

An another thought also made a similar distinction that a person who strives for excellence as one who works hard, feels confident, feels good with a high but not necessarily perfect score, tries something new, takes risks, and learns from success as well as failure experiences. In contrast, if we describe a perfectionist as one who overworks, procrastinates, feels unconfident, feels bad with less-than-perfect scores, and avoids new experiences to prevent making mistakes.

In brief, the striving for excellence is defined as good, desirable, and healthy, but perfectionism is bad, undesirable, and unhealthy as well.

Recent research & studies on perfectionism as striving for excellence in the context of the changing conceptions of perfectionism and the development of new multidimensional perfectionism measures, the findings on the dimensionality and typology of perfectionism as well as the prevalence of perfectionism among gifted students have led to the conclusion that perfectionism can be distinguished into positive and negative dimensions, and that there might be positive as well as negative perfectionists.

Implications of these recent findings for the promotion of positive perfectionism as the striving of excellence amongst the students are discussed worldwide. It is now very popular to distinguish the pursuit of excellence from perfectionism that is defined negatively or in the context of psychopathology.

A perfectionist as an individual “who thinks anything short of perfection in performance is unacceptable” in contrast to defining one who strives for excellence as an individual who is “able to derive personal satisfaction and pride from a good-enough performance”.

Similarly, one who strives for excellence has good self-esteem, strong desires to master a task and do the best, whereas a perfectionist has a need to excel in anxious attempts to bolster flagging self-esteem, suggesting that perfectionism is a psychic wound and is never healthy.

Types of Perfectionism

Following types of perfectionism has been defined for easy understanding:-

- **Objective goods perfectionism:** the most general version of perfectionism, in which the criteria for highest “good” does not depend on human preferences or views. For example, if an objective goods perfectionist believes that scientific development is a “good,” than they mean that it is, period, for all of us, whether we all believe in it or not.
- **Non-humanistic perfectionism**: versions of perfectionism in which the objective “goods” are not all human conditions. Great artistic and scientific accomplishments are among the most often cited non-human perfectionist goods.
- **Humanistic perfectionism**: in which the “goods” are human conditions, such as:-

1. **Personal well-being**: the highest good is the greatest health and happiness of individuals.
2. **Human excellence**: the highest good is the greatest development of human potentials such as athleticism and artistry.

3. **Human nature perfectionism:** the highest good is the fulfillment of either universal or individual human natures, such as the capacities for reason and compassion.

Positive aspect of perfectionism

Perfectionism is viewed and considered as an impactful measure especially in the personality and counseling area. Perfectionism is viewed healthy while the striving for perfection includes social concern along with the maximizing of one's potential. One of the most positive views for perfectionism is described as a process of self-actualization that necessarily involves the struggle for perfection of one's talents and capabilities.

Negative aspect of perfectionism

This conceptualization of perfectionism as negative or pathological has its basis in research studies with adults, and has its roots in clinical observations and studies that associated perfectionism with a host of physical problems, psychological disorders, and psychiatric conditions, specifically, perfectionistic strivings have been suggested to associate with depression, eating disorders, obsessive compulsive disorder, psychosomatic disorders, Type A coronary-prone behavior and suicide. Despite the body of evidence supporting the link, one can argue that such associations do not lead to the conclusion that pathological conditions are directly caused by perfectionism or that perfectionism is inherently destructive. Nonetheless, perfectionism has been linked both to the pursuit of high and unrealistic goals, which could be destructive and compulsive and to a fear of failure and procrastination.

Over the years, this traditional and negative view of perfectionism has not gone unchallenged. Indeed, a positive view of perfectionism has also emerged, especially in the personality and counseling area.

Perfectionism can be viewed as healthy when the striving for perfection includes social concern along with the maximizing of one's potential. Emphasizing on the positive view considering that self-actualization necessarily involves the struggle for perfection of one's talents and capabilities has significant role in pursuing perfection.

Apart from the two somewhat contrasting positions, a **third perspective** has also emerged and has been increasingly adopted by theorists and researchers who view that perfectionism could be represented by a continuum of behaviors and thoughts, and has positive or healthy and negative or unhealthy aspects. Alternatively, it has been suggested that there could be separate positive and negative forms of perfectionism.

This perspective can be represented through dichotomy that distinguishes **normal from neurotic perfectionism.**

Normal perfectionism is characterized by conscientious efforts to strive for excellence on tasks whereas neurotic perfectionism is characterized by neurotic and obsessive-compulsive behaviors in the pursuit.

Further, normal and neurotic perfectionists are also distinguished by their thinking about behaviors. Specifically, normal perfectionists derive great pleasure from accomplishments and allow themselves to fail and to be imperfect, whereas neurotic perfectionists, with their extremely high standards, are preoccupied with avoiding mistakes, and never feel that their efforts are good enough.

In summary, it seems that both normal and neurotic perfectionists could be represented by the striving to meet the high standards they set for themselves, but normal perfectionists are associated with the accommodation of limitations or imperfections and the satisfaction with their best performance whereas neurotic perfectionists are associated with the non-acceptance of imperfections and the dissatisfaction with their best performance.

Accordingly, the striving for excellence is inherent in perfectionism, normal or positive and neurotic or negative alike, and cannot be viewed as the antithesis or opposite of perfectionism.

The development of perfectionism measures running parallel to the evolving conceptualization of perfectionism from a one-dimensional and primarily negative construct to a multidimensional construct with positive and negative aspects, the assessment of perfectionism has progressed from the development of one-dimensional scales to the development of scales that stress the multidimensional nature of the construct.

For example, a one-dimensional scale that assesses perfectionism as a combination of thoughts and behaviors generally associated with excessively high standards or expectations for one's own performance. However, it was the development of multidimensional scales, which provided new impetus to the recent burgeoning (increasing rapidly) of perfectionism research. Specifically, the emphasis on the multidimensional and interpersonal aspects of perfectionism developed 45-item Multidimensional Perfectionism Scale (MPS) that assesses **self-oriented**, **other-oriented**, and **socially prescribed perfectionism**.

Self-oriented perfectionism focuses on excessively high standards, other-oriented perfectionism examines an individual's Perfectionism and the Striving for Excellence 5 expectations of others, and socially-prescribed perfectionism addresses the perceptions of standards set by others. Accordingly, perfectionism not only has an influence on the demands one expects of oneself but also on the demands one expects of others. Other researchers also emphasized the multidimensional nature of perfectionism, and developed a 35-item multidimensional questionnaire. Here Six major dimensions were considered:-

1. Concern over making mistakes,
2. High personal standards,
3. Perception of high parental criticism,
4. Doubting of the quality of one's actions,
5. Perception of high parental expectations,
6. High preference for order and organization.

In brief, there is a collective emphasis on the conceptualization that perfectionism is associated with the setting of very high standards, again suggesting that the striving for excellence is encompassed in the construct of perfectionism.

Further, the Promotion of Positive Perfectionism as the Striving for Excellence Recent research studies on perfectionism have certainly provided new insights as to how educators, teachers, and parents could view perfectionism and work with perfectionist students. The appreciation of the distinction between positive and negative perfectionism and healthy versus unhealthy perfectionists would alert education practitioners to differentiate that not all perfectionistic tendencies are dysfunctional or all perfectionists are unhealthy or maladaptive.

Rather, students with a positive striving for excellence with mastery learning goals should be encouraged. The failure to recognize the positive-negative or healthy-unhealthy distinction might lead to an obstruction of gifted students' striving for excellence, not knowing that these behaviors could be manifestations of adaptive achievement motives and goals. In addition, students, while being helped to set high standards and meet challenging goals with good planning and organization, should also learn to recognize their own limitations and appreciate that their mistakes and failures are normal, informative, and situation-specific, and to derive satisfaction on having performed their best despite that there could still be a discrepancy between their desired standards and their performance.

Furthermore, teachers and parents could share with students their failure experiences and model adaptive coping strategies to tackle situations where a standard-performance discrepancy does occur, or they could also share success experiences and allow students to learn to savor the **pleasure of success** with the understanding that there are limitations and imperfections.

In summary, recent research findings on perfectionism have revealed that it would be more meaningful and beneficial for students to view perfectionism as having positive and negative aspects. The recognition of the distinction will allow one to set high standards and strive for excellence without being trapped in the problems of non-acceptance of imperfections and limitations and dissatisfaction with Perfectionism and the Striving for Excellence is one's best performance.

Thus, the promotion of positive perfectionism will allow one to strive for excellence for the full expression of one's capabilities, whereas eschewing perfectionism because of its negative aspect might lead to a sacrifice of the pursuit of excellence.

Perfectionism - a way of perfect living.

Perfectionism has acquired a number of meanings in human life through contemporary moral and political philosophy. The term is used to refer to an account of a good human life, an account of human well-being, a moral theory, and an approach to politics. Historically, perfectionism is associated with **ethical theories** that characterize the human goodness in terms of the development of human nature that seek to identify the goodness that contribute to the value of a life for human beings.

The good life for human beings can be understood in at least two importantly different ways. On the first understanding, such a life is construed in terms of well-being. The best life for a human being is a life that goes maximally well for the person who leads it. On the second understanding, the good life for a human being is construed in terms of excellence or success. An excellent or perfect human life could be a life that is best in terms of well-being, but it need not be, for it is possible that such a life requires a human being to make sacrifices in his own well-being for the sake of other persons or goods. Thus the notion of an excellent human life is broader than that of a life high in well-being. And since it is the broader notion, a general characterization of perfectionism should employ it rather than well-being.

The best life for a human being is the life that maximizes the development of his nature. Then, it still could be true that for different human beings different activities and pursuits would best promote their goodness. This could be true, since different people may be able to best develop different aspects of human nature. Given their temperament and talents, some do well to concentrate on artistic pursuits, while others do well to focus on theoretical studies or athletic achievements.

Moreover, even those who do well to focus on the same type of perfection. It might be found that some activities and goals serve this end better for them than for others. Finally, different tradeoffs between one's own perfection and the perfection of others may be rationally eligible and this too will contribute to the plurality and variety of modes of life consistent with the perfectionist ideal.

The compatibility of objective goods perfectionism and value pluralism also can be established. One need only assume that some perfectionist goods are either roughly equal or incomparable in values.

Perfection as Self-Regarding duties

As a human being, self-regarding duty to develop one's talents is such a duty, which is categorical. One has the duty whether or not one has a desire to fulfill it.

Human beings, as a community, should take care about **their own perfection** and the **perfection of others** as well. As it is seen, **the standard of perfection** is objective in the sense that it guides, or should guide, human action, even if, what it recommends, is not desired. These claims explain why perfectionism assigns an important place to **self-regarding duties**.

The possibility of self-regarding duties of this kind is sometimes unaccepted or rejected on conceptual grounds.

Moral duties concern one's treatment of others, and so a moral duty to oneself is a confused notion. But this worry should not detain us for a long. The key point is that we can have categorical reasons to develop our nature or to engage in valuable, as opposed to worthless, activities. It is a secondary issue whether we should classify a self-regarding duty as a moral duty or as (merely) a categorical non-moral duty, but while the worry should not detain us, it does point to an attractive feature of perfectionist ethics.

Much contemporary moral theory ignores duties to oneself, whether understood as moral duties or not, and focuses exclusively on our duties toward others. Perfectionist ethics is an important corrective to this tendency. By expanding the domain of ethical concern, it has the potential to enrich contemporary moral philosophy.

Different perfectionist theories offer different accounts of the content of self-regarding duties. Generally speaking, **it is useful to distinguish negative from positive duties** to oneself.

Negative duties are duties to refrain from damaging or destroying one's capacity to lead a good life. For example, barring exceptional circumstances, one has duties to refrain from suicide and self-mutilation.

Positive duties, by contrast, are duties to exercise one's capacity to develop one's nature and / or to realize perfectionist goods. For example, one has a duty to develop one's talents and not to devote one's life entirely to idleness and pleasure.

Specific negative and positive self-regarding duties are derived from the more comprehensive duty to oneself to do what one can to lead a good or excellent life. Stated at this level of abstraction, the perfectionist case for affirming self-regarding duties does not look particularly controversial. Resistance to it will likely derive from one of two quarters. Some will reject the very possibility of categorical duties, whether to oneself or to others. Others will accept the possibility of categorical duties, but insist that they are limited to the treatment of others.

Perfection – an ultimate goal of human beings.

The adjective "**perfect**" when applied to a human life, it means the maximum good or we can say the excellent achievements or attainments of human life that is supposed to be ultimate. **Perfection** related to human nature development having pleasurable sensations or attitudes is to identify goodness and activities that human beings ought to preserve, promote and engage with.

Perfection as a morality should be the core objective of human beings to protect and promote objectively good human lives. Each human being is supposed to perfect himself as much as possible, or at least to some threshold level, at the same time, it is worth mentioning that the good of others contributes substantially to one's own good and by promoting the good of others, one can thereby promote one's own good as well.

This can be considered as one of the most important part of moral responsibility that we must promote our own perfection and the perfection of others as well, whether it takes an egoistic or non-egoistic form, perfectionism is best understood as a moral theory that directs human beings to care about the perfection of others as well as themselves.

Sometimes, we face serious limits to our ability to bring out the perfection of others and we feel resistances in valuable social relationships, but if we can work hard to motivate others by examples that they live under conditions which are conducive to their own self-development or their own realization of perfections, but are not final and can be further enhanced upward, we can be able to convince for the promotion.

This view holds that we should value the perfection of each and every human being, but **in aggregating human perfection we should count the greater perfections simply in virtue of being greater.**

A human life that achieves greater perfections count in virtue of being greater and in virtue of an appropriate multiplier consistently and persistently, an equal unit increase of perfection counts for more the greater the perfection already attained and it becomes the **ultimate goal of human beings.**

Perfection as spiritual attainments

Human beings are spiritual by nature and follow certain spiritual deontology to satisfy their soul for absolute perfection as spiritual attainments, the final goal of human life. It can be achieved through practice towards self-perfection through self-actualization.

Self-actualization refers to the need for personal growth and development that exists throughout the life. If we are self-actualized, we work hard to grow and become who we want to be in life and reach our full potential. If we are an honest person, highly creative, have strong moral/ethical standards, we may be on our way towards achieving self-actualization.

Human motivation is based on an individual's ability to seek fulfillment and change through personal growth. Further, individuals strive for higher needs when their lower-level needs have been fulfilled or satisfied. For example, if we are hungry, we may be too focused on obtaining food (a physiological need) to seek safety or love in our life. On the other hand, when our basic needs of hunger or safety are met we can focus on finding love, our achievements and feeling accomplished in our life, which then leads to the highest level of fulfillment, self-actualization, which means we have reached our full potential in our life.

Characteristics of a Self-Actualized Person

A self-actualized person is someone who feels fulfilled and has accomplished all the things they are capable of accomplishing in their life through personal growth and peak experiences, which are moments of deep meaning or emotion. Here are a few characteristics of a self-actualized person:

1. Problem-centered (not self-centered).
2. Highly creative.
3. Takes responsibility and works hard.
4. Strong moral / ethical standards.
5. Honest and avoids pretense.

Once an individual has reached a sufficiently high level of consciousness & self-knowledge he or she has the capacity both for self-analysis and observation, and also develops the capabilities for understanding the thoughts & actions of others. Motivated by the wish for recognition, acceptance and authority in society, an individual develops personal qualities by **self-perfecting process**.

The systematic improving of qualities and habits of behaviour, whether moral, physical or ethical, constitutes the activity of self-perfection.

The process of **self-perfection** is decidedly the basic concept and leading thread. It is therefore important to understand what it implies. It does not mean developing one's talents or attaining perfect mastery of some technical ability only. There are many different ways of improving one's physical or mental skills; but when it comes to **spirituality**, it is the very essence of human nature which is the main issue.

The purpose of spirituality is not merely to develop physical and mental faculties, but to bring one's essential self to full **spiritual maturity**. On a different level, the aim of an individual on a spiritual path such as yoga is also self-perfection.

In the quest for self-perfection for spiritual attainments, humans have always desired knowledge to develop the ability to pursue the passions. Without passion there would be no reason to pursue increased knowledge, and our reason and understanding would thus be incomplete to acquire the perfectibility.

Each successful decision assures humans of their own unique abilities, and this self-assurance leads to **self-empowerment**. Humans, in their quest for **"perfectibility"** realize their authority. Indeed, **self-perfection grants power, and the domination of nature may well be the ultimate ability.**

Humans also recognize this desire for **self-perfection** in other individuals, and in some cases respect those that are attempting great feats in the name of development.

Further, the ability to choose, irrespective of nature, to promote one's own **self-perfection** is distinctively human. Animals lack this drive for self-perfection.

The pursuit of one human's unique desire, passion for knowledge, compassion for others, and love leads to self-perfection, which ensures the enhancement of all other capabilities and **spirituality of his soul is ensured to attain the absolute perfection.**

Highlights

- *Anything having its **highest level of attainment is perfection**.*
- ***Perfection in human life** is all about the perfect alignment of Body, Mind and Soul.*
- ***Perfection is an action, an activity, a pursuit, not a thing or static state**.*
- *Perfection is a destination to go through the small steps of performances and subsequent gradual successes.*
- *Perfectionism is pursuing the best possible human life with excellence, ethics or politics that prioritize goals of good living.*
- *In **ethics** and value theory, **perfectionism** is the persistence of **will** in obtaining the optimal quality of **spiritual, mental, physical, and material being**.*
- ***Perfectionism** can be described as an account of the good life, or the intrinsically desirable life.*
- ***Perfectionism is a way of perfect living, perfection is to attain physical, mental and spiritual maturity in life.***
- ***Perfection** related to human nature development having pleasurable sensations or attitudes is to*

identify goodness and activities that human beings ought to preserve, promote and engage with.

- ***In aggregating human perfection we should count the greater perfections simply in virtue of being greater.***

A BRIEF PROFESSIONAL INTRODUCTION ABOUT THE AUTHOR

Binay Kumar Jha
Vice President
Mob: +91 8860018279, 7975532924

ECOTECH
Automotive Innovation

ECOTECH MACHINERIES
A Complete Garage Solutions

Corporate Office: E-69, Jasola Village, Mother Dairy Road, Nr. Metro Pillar No-139, Jasola, New Delhi - 110025
Regional Office: 117/3, Suraj Nagar, Nr. Tagore Public School, Kanadia Road, Bangali Square, Indore - 452016 (M.P)
Email: vp.binayjha@ecotechmachineries.com | **Web:** www.ecotechmachineries.com
Helpline No.: +91 9911 61 7384, +91 9911 61 7385

TOYOTA

BINAY KUMAR JHA
General Manager (Service Planning)

UTTAM TOYOTA

• DELHI • NOIDA • GHAZIABAD • SAHIBABAD

Amiantit Oman

Binay Kumar Jha
Deputy General Manager
(Engineering Services Division)

Amiantit Oman Company LLC
(An ISO 9001, 14001 & OHSAS 18001 Company)
P.O. Box: 417, Postal Code 111, Rusayl, Sultanate of Oman
Tel.: +968 24449800, 24445830 Ext:152, Dir:24445865, Fax: 24446611, GSM: 99330251
Email: jha_amiantit@omzest.com, esd_amiantit@omzest.com
Website: www.amiantitoman.com
| HDPE | ROTOMOULD | CONCRETE | PVC | GRP | GRC |
Leaders in Pipes, Infrastructure & Moulded Products

H

Binay Kumar Jha
Vice President

Hindfibro Pvt. Ltd.
201, Crowne Heights,
Hotel Crowne Plaza, Rohini, Sec-10,
Delhi-110085

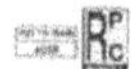

Mob. : 9818389233
9212313843

Binay Kr. Jha
Plant Head

Royal Pressing & Components Pvt. Ltd.
I-36, Site-C, (U.P.S.I.D.C.), Surajpur Dadri Road,
Surajpur, Greater Noida (U.P.)
E-mail : royalmulti@rediffmail.com
jha_saab@rediffmail.com
Phone : 0120-2569565, 2560194

QS 9000 : 1998
ISO 9001 : 1998
CERTIFIED FIRM

BINAY KUMAR JHA
General Manager - Works

Hindustan Composites Ltd.
(An ISO 9001 : 2000 Company)
Plot No. D-2/1, MIDC Indl. Area,
Paithan, Dist. Aurangabad - 431 148.
Web Site - www.hindcompo.com

Tel. D. (02431) 233464,
Telefax (02431) 232063,
Mobile : 9764444073
E-mail: jha_saab@rediffmail.com
binayjha1966@gmail.com

BINAY KUMAR JHA
General Manager

PARISHUDH MACHINES PVT. LTD.
(AUTOPARTS DIVISION)
B-14, Industrial Area, Meerut Road,
Ghaziabad - 201 003 INDIA
Phones : +91 120 2714741, 2712266
Fax : (0091 120) 2714111 Mob. : 9811103951
E-mail : gainol@vsnl.com, jha_saab@rediffmail.com

BINAY KUMAR JHA
General Manager (Engg.)

ROTO PUMPS LTD.
B-15, Phase-II Extn., NOIDA - 201 305 (U.P.) India
Tel : (+91) (0120) 3043945 / 946 / 947 / 948, Direct : 3043981
Fax : (+91) (0120) 2567967, 3043988
e-mail : bkjha@rotopumps.com
Website : www.rotopumps.com

Binay Kumar Jha

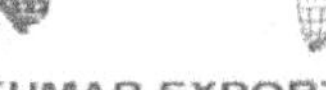

KUMAR EXPORTS
C-180, Phase VI, Focal Point, Ludhiana-141010 (India)
MFRS. & EXPORTERS OF AUTO PARTS, CASTINGS & GRADED FASTNERS

Binay Kr. Jha
(General Manager)

Spectra Products Pvt. Ltd.
F-6, Sector-17, Kavi Nagar, Industrial Area, Ghaziabad-201 002 (U.P.) INDIA
Tel. (O) 91-120-2701261, 2702826 Fax 91-120-2789023 91-11-79538784
E-mail bjha@specpro.com Mobile 33339183

www.ingramcontent.com/pod-product-compliance
Ingram Content Group UK Ltd.
Pitfield, Milton Keynes, MK11 3LW, UK
UKHW021648190726
13853UKWH00001B/120